THE SUN UNWOUND

THE SUN UNWOUND

ORIGINAL TEXTS FROM OCCUPIED AMERICA

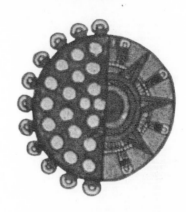

WITH ENGLISH TRANSLATIONS BY EDWARD DORN AND GORDON BROTHERSTON

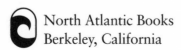

North Atlantic Books
Berkeley, California

The Sun Unwound
Original Texts from Occupied America

Published by
North Atlantic Books
P.O. Box 12327
Berkeley, California 94712

Cover art from Borbonicus Codex p. 11
Cover and book design by Paula Morrison

Printed in the United States of America

The Sun Unwound is sponsored by the Society for the Study of Native Arts and Sciences, a nonprofit educational corporation whose goals are to develop an educational and crosscultural perspective linking various scientific, social, and artistic fields; to nurture a holistic view of arts, sciences, humanities, and healing; and to publish and distribute literature on the relationship of mind, body, and nature.

Library of Congress Cataloging-in-Publication Data

The sun unwound : poems from occupied America / edited by Edward Dorn
   and Gordon Brotherston.
        p.   cm.
   Spanish poems include Spanish original and English translation.
   Anthology of Nahuatl, Mayan, Quechua, and Spanish poems
   ISBN 1-55643-292-5
     1. America—Poetry.   2. Latin America—Poetry.   I. Dorn, Edward.
II. Brotherston, Gordon.
PN6110.P7A467   1998
808.81'9321812—dc21   98-19843
                                                                    CIP

1   2   3   4   5   6   7   8   9/ 03   02   01   00   99

Table of Contents

IMAGES OF THE NEW WORLD

Nahuatl

Maya

PALABRA DE GUERRILLERO

MODERN CHRONICLES

César Vallejo, Peru
Selected Poems

Preface

In gathering translations of texts from diverse sources, *The Sun Unwound* finds its focus in America, in three successive stages. The principle and beginning are given by the first settlers of the continent, statements in Nahuatl, Maya and Quechua which, with intellectual authority, gauge the cultural depth of Mesoamerica and the Andes, as well as the disastrous consequences of the European invasions. This is the tradition that most intricately articulates time with sun, specificially the "suns" or more ancient creations which inhere in our time, the "tonatiuh" of flood, eclipse, volcanic rain and hurricane described in the Nahuatl genesis. In Chimalpahin's Nahuatl reworking of 16th-century European geography, these suns also come to be spread terrestrially as the four worlds of the planet, in a system which acknowledges America's equal rights to its own past and future. Many of these native American pieces appeared in reviews and journals from the late 1960s on, and, after greater or lesser revisions, were almost all included in *Image of the New World. The American Continent portrayed in Native Texts* (Thames & Hudson 1979).

Faith in the idea of an America liberated from its worst European imposition militantly informs the second and central phase of this continental story, represented here by pieces published in 1968 under the title *Our Word/Palabra de guerrillero* (Cape Goliard). Stemming again in the main from Mesoamerica (Guatemala, Nicaragua) and the Andes, these texts tell, first-hand and in the first person, of the great guerrillero revolution of the mid 20th century, which triumphed in Cuba in 1959. The violence and sadism sent to counter that movement had silenced most of the guerrillero poets by the time *Our Word* appeared. Javier Heraud (Peru) was shot down, aged 21, in 1963. The year 1967 saw the end of three of them: Otto René Castillo (Guatemala), tortured for four days and then burnt; Fernando Gordillo (Nicaragua); and Che Guevara (Argentina/Cuba), whose example easily survives all derogation.

The first chronicle belongs to the Peruvian César Vallejo (1892–1938). The greatest poet in modern Spanish, he was born of half-Indian parents in the small northern town of Santiago de Chuca. He did his time in prison when he was a student at the University in Lima. Vallejo's "human poems"—to use the title of his most substantial volume—have few if any rivals for the way they diagnose American racism and economic butchery, finding out of all this a place for the Indian who is "before and after man." The poem from which this last phrase is taken, "Bedrock and Lode" ("Telúrica y magnética"), discovers in the Andean cordillera a millennial American stratigraphy, and a sharp atmosphere that is the "solar and nourishing absence of sea,/and oceanic sentiment in everything." Like Pagú's work, "Bedrock and Lode" was especially translated for this volume (The other poems originally appeared in *César Vallejo: Selected Poems*, Penguin 1976).

The inclusion of the great Brazilian socialist Patricia Galvão (Pagú) (1910–62), was prompted by the screening at the 1989 Havana International Film Festival of Norma Bengell's film *Eternamente Pagú* (1987). A leading and flamboyant member of the vanguardist movement in São Paulo during the thirties, she was also militant in her political dedication, especially in her concern for working women's rights—the subject of her novel, *Industrial Park* (1933). That same year she went to Manchuria as a journalist to cover the Russo/Japanese War. She became a close friend of the prince and presumed heir to the throne, and upon her departure he gave her rare seeds and plants, some of which enriched the Brazilian economy. She was imprisoned and tortured under the Vargas dictatorship between 1935 and 1940, but despite her ruined health, continued her political and literary activities for two more decades.

The versions offered here of her illustrated *Album* (1929), written when she was nineteen, and her late poems (published in *A Tribuna*, the Santos newspaper, 1960–1962) owe much to the knowledge and cooperation of Lúcia Sá and have not appeared before. Undoubtedly the most neglected and abandoned of all the major creators of her time, her luminous intelligence was celebrated in solar terms in Augusto de Campos's "Ofertorio":

> Sun, mirror of the sun, other sun, doña sun.
> Opponent of the sun, sower of beauties
> Hard bright assault against my eyes, a lake.

Pacify me, rude as I am, aurora
Born, feed me on gold
Twin of light
& SUN

The chronicles with which *The Sun Unwound* concludes reflect on the same experience in "modern" terms, each being consciously set within the politics and possibilities of nation states. The piece by José Emilio Pacheco (1939–) is from *Los elementos de la noche* (1963) and was published by Black Sparrow Press in 1968 as *Tree between Two Walls*. An early work, it sets up the counterpoint that runs through Pacheco's poetry, that agonic pull between the ancient time of "unwinding suns" (his phrase) and modern urban Mexico.

These versions aim neither to be tied down to nor to replace their originals. For that reason we have made a point of including those originals, not just in the case of the imported languages Spanish and Portuguese but of such predecessors as Nahuatl, Maya and Quechua. The inclusion of cognate examples of American visual language stems from the same desire to recognize the existence of literary space that is not just gratuitous, decorative accompaniment.

The collaboration which produced this work began in the Department of Literature, University of Essex, in 1967 and continued on one or other side of the North Atlantic for more than a decade. Preparing this volume became the spur for further translation and certain minimal revisions. Throughout, the care given by Jennifer Dunbar has been indispensable.

GB/ED
March 1998

IMAGES
OF THE
NEW WORLD

NAHUATL

The Suns

Y ynic ce tonatiuh onmanca yn itzinecan
4 atl yn itonal
mitoa atonatiuh
yn ipan in ye yquac
yn mochih yn atocoac
Yn aneneztihuac
yn tlaca michtihuac

Y ynic ome tonatiuh onmanca
4 ocelotl yn itonal catca
motenehua ocelotonatiuh
ypan mochiuh
tlapachiuh yn ylhuicatl
yn tonatiuh yn yquac amo otlatocaya
can nepantla tonatiuh mochihua
niman tlayohuaya
yn onotloyohuac niman tequaloya
auh ypan inyn quinametin nemia
conitotihui yn huehuetque
yn netlapaloliz catca ma timohuetzit
ypampa yn aquin huetzia
yccen huetzia

Y ynic ey tonatiuh onmanca
4 quiyahuitl yn itonal
mitoa quiyauhtonatiuh
ypan ynyn mochiuh yn ipan tlequiauh
y onocca yc tlatlaque
yhuan ypan xaltequiyauh conytohua yquac motepeuh
yn xaltetl yn ticytta
yhuan popozocac yn tezontli
yhuan yquac momaman yn texcalli chichichiliuhticac

The Suns

The first sun to be founded
has the Sign Four Water,
it is called Water Sun.
Then it happened
that water carried everything away
everything vanished
the people were changed into fish.

The second sun to be founded
has the Sign Four Jaguar,
it is called Jaguar Sun.
Then it happened
that the sky collapsed
the Sun did not follow its course at midday
immediately it was night
and when it grew dark
the people were torn to pieces.
In this Sun giants lived.
The old ones said
the giants greeted each other thus:
"Don't fall over," for whoever fell,
fell forever.

The third sun to be founded,
the Sign Four Rain
is called Rain Sun.
It happened then that fire rained down,
all who lived there were burned.
They say that then tiny stones rained down and spread
the fine stones that we can see
the tezontli boiled into stone
and the reddish rocks were twisted up.

Y ynic 4 tonatiuh
4 ecatl ytonal
mitoa ecatonatiuh
ypan in ecatocoac ozomatihuac
quauhtla quin tepehuato yn onocca
tlacaozomatin

Y ynic maculilli tonatiuh
4 ollin yn itonal
mitoa olintonatiuh
ypanpa molini yn otlatoca
auh yn yuh conitotihui yn huehuetque
ypan inyn mochihuaz tlalloliniz mayanaloz
ynic tipolihuizque

The fourth sun
Sign Four Wind,
is called Wind Sun.
Then the wind carried everything away.
The people all turned into monkeys
and went to live in the forests.

The fifth Sun,
Sign Four Ollin,
is called Earthquake Sun
because it started into motion.
The old ones said
in this Sun there will be earthquakes and general hunger
from which we shall perish.

Quetzalcoatl, Lord of the Dawn

niman quimilhui yni tecpoyohuan
Ma ixquichcocol tecpoyotl matihui yan nohuian xictzahaquacan
xictlatican yn oticmexyioca yn paquiliztli yn necuiltonolli yn yxquich
taxcato tlatqui auh yni tecpoyohuan yuhquilichiuloque oncantlatl-
atique yni nealtiayan catca quetzalcoatl yn ytoca yocan atecpan
amochco niman yc ya yn quetzalcoatl moquehqui cenpoh yni tecpoy-
ohuan quianchoquilli

niman yaque ompatlamatiaque yn tlillan in tlapallan intlatlayan
auh nahuianquitytia moyeyecotia acantlahualittac

auh yn oacic yn ompa tlamatihuia niman occeppa oncan chocac
tlaocox ye ypan ynyn xihuitl ce acatl motenehua mitoa yniquac oac-
ito teoapan ylhuicaatenco niman moquetz chocac concuic yn itlatqui
mochichiuh yn yapanecayouh yn ixiuhxayac auh yn iquac omocen-
cauh niman yc ynomatca motlati motlecahui yc motocayotia yn tlat-
layan yn ompa motlatito yn quetzalcoatl

auh mitoa yn iquac yn ye tlatla niman ye ic aco quiza yn inexyo
auh yn neciya yn quittaya mochi tlazototome yn aco quiza yn ilhuicac
quimonitta tlauhquechol xiuhtototl tzinitzcan ayoquan tozneneme
allome cochome yxquich yn oczequi tlazototome auh yn ontlan
ynexyo niman ye ic aco quiza yn iyollo quetzaltototl yn quitta auh
yn iuh quimatia ylhuicac ya ylhuicac callac quitohuaya yn huehuetque
yehuatl yn mocuep yn citlallin yn tlahuizcalpan hualneci yn iuh quitoa
yniquac necico yn mic quetzalcoatl ye quitocayotiaya tlahuizcal-
panteuctli

yniquac mic zan nahuilhuitl yn amo nez yc quitoaya yniquac mic
can nahuilhuitli yn amo nez quitohuaya yquac mictlan nemito auh
no nahuilhuitl momiti yc chicueylhuitlica yn necico huey citlalin yn
quitoaya quetzalcoatl quitoaya yquac moteuctlalli auh yn iuh quima-
tia yniquac hualneztiuh yntleyn ypan tonalli cecentlamantin ypan
miyotia quinmina quintlahuelia

Quetzalcoatl, Lord of the Dawn

Then he said to his heralds:
"Before we go, on every side conceal and bury what we have made here, joy and wealth, the whole of our possession." And his heralds did so. They hid everything there, in the place where Quetzalcoatl bathed, which was called Atecpan, Water Palace, Amochco, Tin Place. And Quetzalcoatl left. He stood up, summoned his heralds and wept over them.

They then set off searching for the place of the Black and the Red, the place of Incineration. And they traveled and wandered far, nowhere pleased them.

When they reached the place they were searching for, now again there he wept and suffered. In this year 1 Reed (so it is told, so it is said), when he had reached the ocean shore, the edge of the sky-water, he stood up, wept, took his attire, and put on his plumes, his precious mask. When he was dressed, of his own accord he burnt himself, he gave himself to the fire. So that where Quetzalcoatl burnt himself is called the place of Incineration.

And it is said that when he burned, his ashes rose up and every kind of precious bird appeared and could be seen rising up to the sky: roseate spoonbill, cotinga, trogon, blue heron, yellow-headed parrot, macaw, white-fronted parrot, and all other precious birds. And after he had become ash the quetzal bird's heart rose up; it could be seen and was known to enter the sky. The old men would say he had become Venus; and it is told that when the star appeared Quetzalcoatl died. From now on he was called the Lord of the Dawn.

Only for four days he did not appear, so it is told, and dwelt in Dead Land. And for another four days he sharpened himself. After eight days the great star appeared called Quetzalcoatl on his ruler's throne. And they knew, on his rising, which people, according to Sign, he penetrates, shoots into and loathes.

Quetzalcoatl Goes to the Underworld

And thereupon the gods conferred and said:
"Who now shall be alive?
Heaven is founded, earth is founded,
who now shall be alive, oh gods?"
They were sorrowful:
Star Skirt and Milky Way,
and (with them) the Bridger, the Emerger,
the Earth-firmer, the Tiller;
Quetzalcoatl whom we serve.

And then Quetzalcoatl goes to Mictlan, the Dead Land.
He approached the Lord and Lady of Mictlan and said:
"What I have come for is the precious bones which you possess;
I have come to fetch them."
And he was asked:
"What do you want to do with them, Quetzalcoatl?"
And he answered:
"What worries the gods is who shall live on earth."
And the Lord of Mictlan then said:
"All right. Blow this conch and carry the bones four times round
    my jade circle."
But the conch is totally blocked up.
Quetzalcoatl summons the worms, they hollow it out.
The large and the small bees force their way through.
He blows it; the sound reaches the Lord of Mictlan.

And the Lord of Mictlan next said to him:
"All right, take them."
But to his vassals, the Micteca, he said:
"Tell him, oh gods, he should leave them here."
But Quetzalcoatl answered:
"No; I'm taking them with me."
And then his nahual said to him:

"Just tell them: 'I've left them here.'"
And so he said, he shouted to them:
"I have left them here."
But then he really went back up, clutching the precious bones,
male bones on one side, female on the other.
He took them and wrapped them up, and took them with him.
And the Lord of Mictlan again spoke to his vassals:
"Oh gods, is Quetzalcoatl really taking the bones? Dig him a pit."
They dug him one; he stumbled and fell in.
And Quails menaced him and he fainted.
He dropped the precious bones and the Quails tore and pecked at
    them.
And then Quetzalcoatl came to and weeps and says to his nahual:
"Oh my nahual, what now?"
And the reply came:
"What now? Thing went badly; let it be."
And then he gathered the bits, took them and wrapped them in a
    bundle
which he took to Tamoanchan.
When he had brought it there it was ground up by the
woman named Quilaztli, that is, Cihuacohuatl.
Then she placed the meal in a jade bowl and Quetzalcoatl
    dropped blood on it by piercing his member.
Then all the gods named here did penance like
the Bridger, the Tiller,
the Emerger, the Earth-firmer,
the Plunger, the Shooter:
Quetzalcoatl.
And they said:
"The servants of the gods are born." For indeed they did penance
    for us.
Then they said:
"What shall they eat? The gods must find food."
And the ant fetched
the maize kernels from the heart of the Food Mountain.

Florentine Codex

Good Times at Tula

the toltecs were certainly rich
food was not scarce enough to sell
their vegetables were large
gourds for example mostly too fat to get your arms round
maize ears millstone size
and they actually *climbed*
        their amaranth plants
cotton came ready dyed
in colours like crimson saffron pink violet leaf-green azure
        verdigris orange umbra grey rose-red and coyote yellow
it all just grew that way

they had all kinds of valuable birds
blue cotingas quetzals turpials red-spoonbills
which could talk and sang in tune
jade and gold were low-priced popular possessions
they had chocolate too, fine cocoa flowers everywhere

the toltecs did not in fact lack anything
no one was poor or had a shabby house
and the smaller maize ears they used as fuel
to heat their steam baths with

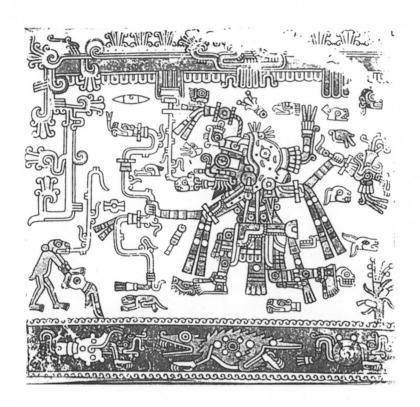

Twenty Sacred Hymns

Tlaloc

CHORUS

In Mexico the god is being asked for a loan
among the paper banners in four directions
now is the time for weeping

PRIEST

I am prepared   I take to the courtyard
the bundles of bloodthorns of my god
you are my commander magic prince
and you are the one who makes our flesh
you are the very first one   the offerings
can only cause you shame

TLALOC   But if someone causes me shame
           it is because he didn't know me
           you are my fathers my elder priesthood
           the Jaguar Snake
           the Jaguar Snake

PRIEST   From Tlalocan in a jade boat
           Acatonal comes out
           extend yourself in Poyauhtlan
           with rattles of mist he is taken to Tlalocan

VICTIM   *My brother, Tozcuecuexi,*
           I am going forever it's the time of weeping
           send me to wherever it is
           under his command   I have already said
           to the frightening prince I am going forever
           it is time for weeping
           over four years we shall be carried on the wind
           unknown to others by you it is told
           to the place of the unfleshed
           In the house of Quetzal plumes
           transformation is effected
           it is the due of the one who vivifies men

CHORUS   Extend yourself in Poyauhtlan
           with rattles of mist he is taken to Tlalocan

Huitzilopochtli

Hymn of the one born on his shield and the motherhood of the earth.

The great war lord has burst from Earth's swollen belly born on his shield.

The great war lord has burst from Earth's swollen belly born on his shield.

Astride the Snake Hill he triumphs,
between the pyramids,
with his face-paint on and his shield teueuelli.
No one is so potent as he
And the Earth quivers.

Who else can assume his face-paint and his shield?

Tratado

Peyote Cure

tlacuel tlaxihuallauh xoxouhqui cihuatl
tla xicpehuiti xoxouhqui totonqui yayauhqui totonqui
tlatlauhqui totonqui cocauhqui totonqui
ye oncan nimitztlitan chicomoztoc
amo quin moztla amo quin huiptla
niman axcan ticquixtiz
ac teotl ac mahuiztli
in ye quixpolloa motlachihualtzin
nomatca nehuatl ninahualteuctli

Peyote Cure

Hey, come along, green woman;
scare, scare the green fever, the blackish fever,
the red fever, the yellow fever:
I have already sent you to the Seven Caves.
Not tomorrow nor the day after,
but right now you will make him leave.
What god, what prodigy,
thinks to destroy your creature?
The lord of magic is me and me alone.

Tula Lament

At Tula stood the beamed sanctuary,
only the snake columns still stand,
our prince Nacxitl has gone, has moved away.
     Our vanguard is wept for with conches;
5   he is going to his destruction in Tlapallan.

He was there in Cholula,
made an end at Mount Poyauhtecatitlan,
crossed the water at Acallan.
     Our vanguard is wept for with conches;
10   he is going to his destruction in Tlapallan.

I come to the frontier with winged finery,
the lord who pierces and the victim.
     My fine-plumed lord has gone away
     has left me, 10-Flower, an orphan.

15   The pyramid burst apart hence my tears
the sacred sand whirled up hence my desolation.
     My fine-plumed lord has gone away
     has left me, 10-Flower, an orphan.

Tlapallan is where you are expected
20   is where you are destined to rest;
you are moving on, my fine-plumed lord,
destined for Xicalanco.
Still yet, still yet ...

     Your house will always be there, your gates
25   your palace will always be there.
     You left them orphaned here at the Tula frontier.

You wept endlessly, great lord;
  Your house will always be there, your gates
  your palace will always be there.
30   You left them orphaned here at the Tula frontier.

Stone and wood, you painted them
in the city of Tula.
  Where you ruled, our prince Nacxitl,
  your name will never be destroyed;
35   your people will always cry for you.

The turquoise house and the snake house, you built them
in the city of Tula.
  Where you ruled, our prince Nacxitl,
  your name will never be destroyed;
40   your people will always cry for you.

As white and yellow maize I am born,
The many-coloured flower of living flesh rises up
and opens it glistening seeds before the face of our mother.
In the moisture of Tlalocan, the quetzal water-plants open
        their corollas.
45   I am the work of the only god, his creation.

  Your heart lives in the painted page,
  you sing the royal fibres of the book,
  you make the princes dance,
    there you command by the water's discourse.
50 He created you,
  he uttered you like a flower,
  he painted you like a song:
  a Toltec artist.
  The book has come to the end:
55 your heart is now complete.

Here through art I shall live for ever.
Who will take me, who will go with me?
Here I stand, my friends.
A singer, from my heart I strew my songs,
60 my fragrant songs before the face of others.
I carve a great stone, I paint thick wood
my song is in them.
It will be spoken of when I have gone.
I shall leave my song-image on earth.
65   My heart shall live, it will come back,
      my memory will live and my fame.
I cry as I speak and discourse with my heart.
Let me see the root of song,
let me implant it here on earth so it may be realized.
70   My heart shall live, it will come back,
      my memory will live and my fame.
The Prince Flower gently breathes his aroma,
our flowers are uniting.
      My song is heard and flourishes.
75   My implanted word is sprouting,
      our flowers stand up in the rain.
The Cocoa flower gently opens his aroma,
the gentle Peyote falls like rain.
      My song is heard and flourishes.
80   My implanted word is sprouting,
      our flowers stand up in the rain.

Flower Song

nichuana teihuinti xochitl
yehcoc ye nican poyoma
xahuallan timaliuhtihuitz
maxochitl oyehcoc ye nican
zan tlaahuixochitla moyahua
motzetzeloa ancazo yehuatl nepapan xochitl
       zan comoni huehuetl maya nehtotilo
in quetzalpoyomatl a ic icuilihuic noyol, nicuicanitl
in xochitl a ya tzetzelihuipancuel nicuiya, maxonahuiacan
zan noyolitic ontlapani in cuicaxochitl
nicyamoyahua in xochitlacuicatl
ninoquinilotehuaz in quenmanian
     xochineneliuhtiaz noyollo
     yehuan tepilhuan in tetecutin
zan ye ic nichoca in quenmanian
zan nicayaihtoa noxoichiteyo nocuicatoca
nictalitehuaz in quenmanian
     xochineneliuhtiaz noyollo
     yehuan tepilhuan in tetecutin

Flower Song

I am drinking the liquor of the flower
the narcosis is here
switch into it
the flowers are here in your hands
the flowers of pleasure spread
so shaken in themselves each is iridescent
                    the drum is a growing intrusion, dance
exquisite narcosis stains my heart, the singer's
I bear the iridescent downpour, receive it
just inside my heart the song-flower snapped
I disperse the flower-song
I am going to be frozen in rapture sometime
        my heart will be mixed with the flowers
        and *Les fleurs nobles,* corolla of the Princes
I could cry over the "sometime"
I tell my flower fame, my song name
I'll be somnambulant sometime
        my heart will be mixed with the flowers
        and *Les fleurs nobles,* corolla of the Princes

War Song

quauhyotica oceloyotica
ma onnequechnahualo antepilhuani
ycahcahuanca yn chimallin
cohua ma'limani
zan topan moyahuaya topan tzetzelihuia
ne'calizxochitli yahuiltiloca
ycahcahuanca

yn pozoniya ye onca za miliniya yn tlachinolliya
nemahuizzotiloya nechimaltocayotilco
a oyohualpan teuhtlan motecaya
yaoxochitl mani yeehuaya ato ya tempa
in on cuepontimanique oceloxochitlin chimalli xochitli
a oyohualpan teuhtlan motecaya

yn quauhtehuehueltica ocelopanitli nepanihui yeehuaya
quetzallin chimaltica ye onnemamanalo zaquanpanitl huitoliuhon
pozonia ye oncano hualehuaya
yn chalcatl oo amaqueme oo ayohuilo
yhcahuaca yaoyotl ohuaya ohuaya
yn tlacotl xaxamacatoa
itztlin teytimanio
chimalteuhtli topania motecaya
ho hualehuaya yn chalcatl oo amaqueme oo

War Song

Between the Eagles and the Jaguars
let the embrace happen, oh princes.
To the clash of shields
the Capturers join company.
5   The battle blossom spreads over us and rains down
in godly delight.

There, the blaze seethes and streams along:
ambition to fulfil and shield-fame to win
dust rises over the bells.
10   The war-flower will never end.
Jaguar-Flower and the shield Flower
open their corollas,
dust rises over the bells.

With the Eagle bucklers the Jaguar banner entwine;
15   with the quetzal shields the gold-black banners mingle.
There they seethe and turn.
The Chalcan and the Amecamecan arise,
the clash of war turns around
The arrow shattered,
20   the obsidian splintered:
the shield-dust covers us,
the Chalcan and the Amecamecan arise.

Chimalpahin

Emperors

13 Flint (1440). This was the year Itzcohuatzin died, the ruler of Tenochtitlan, who had governed for 14 years. He was the bastard son of Acamapichtli, who had been the first ruler of Tenochtitlan. And they say the woman who was his mother came to Azcapotzalco as a seller of herbs. Even though her son was not legitimate, he became the great Itzcohuatzin. By then, his father Acamapichtli had been dead for 45 years.

Itzcohuatzin waged war mainly with the help of his nephew, Tlacaeleltzin. They fought and subjected Azcapotzalco, Coyoacan, Xochimilco, and Cuitlahuacan. Tlacaeleltzin was an enterprising campaigner; and although he did not seek civil power in Tenochtitlan, he acquired the insignia of a great man, he increased his estate and enjoyed a rich life.

Next there reigned five other great rulers in Mexico Tenochtitlan: the great Moctezuma Ilhuicamina; Axayacatl; Tizoc; Ahuitzotl, and Moctezuma, the last of the line, in whose reign the Spaniards appeared. These were the great rulers who made themselves feared on every side. But the one who won the highest and the most renown was the captain and war-maker Tlacaeleltzin, as will be seen in these annals. It was he who was able to change the devil Huitzilopochtli into the god of the Mexicans, by the power of his persuasion.

4 House (1509). In this year there was a rebellion in Chalco. When they arrived from Tenochtitlan, Moctezuma's envoys spoke as follows to the rebels: "We are sent here by you lord Tetzahuitl Huitzilopochtli whose breath is in the rushes and in the reeds and who has let this be known: 'Say to Necuametl and his uncle Itzcahua that I will certainly take over this little bit more for Mexico Tenochtitlan; war is certainly said somehow to be dying out now, altogether.'"

Famine

The year 1 Rabbit, 1454. In this year of disaster there was widespread death and thirst. And then there arrived, to stuff themselves in Chalco, frightful packs of boars, poisonous snakes, and vultures as well. And the hunger was so great that the imperial Mexicans sold themselves, and others hid themselves away in the forest, where they lived as wood people. In that region there was nothing to eat for all of four years, so that two separate parties of the Mexicans sold themselves into slavery. It was mainly to buy slaves that the Totonacs came to Mexico with maize, and it was from Cuextlan that they brought it. Before that the Mexicans had not used maize to make loaves. They crawled into holes and died anywhere. The vultures then ate them, and no one buried them. It was every man for himself.

It was also in this year the Texcocans came to build the aqueduct at Chapultepec. It was commissioned by Nezahualcoyotl, the ruler of Colhuacan, so that water would come to Mexico-Tenochtitlan and serve his uncle, the great ruler Moctezuma I, Ilhuicaminatzin ("guardian of the sky").

The Four Continents

Here begins the account
of the world
and its divisions.

Of Europa

One can now see that the world
the Earthe
from Then until Now
is composed of four parts.
May those who see this book know
in the first place stands Europa

and secondly comes Asia
and the third is Africa
and the fourth is Nuevo Mundo
which means the New World.
The size of these four lands is truly enormous.

In Europa there are to be found
great principalities and dukedoms
and great communities which are called provinces.

How many?

There is Spain, France,
Italy, Germany
and Greece, Hungary, Poland,
Sweden and Norway
the ancient home of the Goths.
And then Flanders, and England
which is separated from the others
by a sea channel.

Of Asia

And the second world
is the land called Asia.
The owners of the books
always designated it thus
because it was there
that power had its origin

How many were their dominions?

The Assyrians held sway there,
and Persians and Medes,
but the Christian accounts also record
how our reverenced God
cast the first man, Adam

and the dear Christ, our savior
who, through his unflinching clarity
redeemed us.

Moreover, all
these Christian accounts
were written and compiled long ago
in these lands—
the Testaments Old and New.

Asia is divided into five parts
corresponding to the five great powers
which persist to this day.

The first of these is close to Europa
and is ruled by the Gran Duque
in the city called Moscow.

In the second place another great ruler
bears the name Gran Chan, Emperador
in the country of the Tartars.

In the third place, there is a ruler
who is said to be the one who works as a slaver
for everyone, a truly great ruler
known as the Turk.
In his country is the Holy Land
the place designed by God, Jerusalem.

In the fourth place dwells
the great ruler Sophy Rey
in Persia.
The western limits of his land
border the realm of the Turks
and thus, they are always at war.

The fifth and most remote part of Asia

is La India de Portugal
and the country called Gran China.

Of Africa

The third world is the land named Africa,
which is also divided and in our time, it is mapped
by the scholars of the sky and earthe
called Geografers.

Those who read this book should know
in the first place is Barbary
the land of the Moors
which lies opposite Spain,
and various principalities
are found there: Fez, Morocco, Tunis
and Tlemcen.

In the second place is Numidia
which is a land where few live
because it is not fruitful
but, all the same, in this principality
there is a fruit called Tamarind
and it thrives there as it does elsewhere.

The tamarinds are born on the palm tree
and are called Datiles in Spanish
and they are pleasing
to the eye and the tongue.

In the third place
is the land called Libya
which means *by-the-wood*
or *near-the-grass,* or perhaps
by-the-desert
because that is what is there.
It is especially notable

for its great steppe
of grassland and desert
which is without population like the sea—
it is just wasteland, now unoccupied.

In the fourth division the black man lives
the Negro
who are spread over
as much as a thousand leagues.
They are found all the way to the far shore
where the Cabo Verde begins
and as far as the Cabo de Buena Esperanza.

And in the fifth place
is the land of Egypt.
Although it is small
there are concentrated rich places
watered by the river Nile.
In this land is the great city Cairo
and long before it was Babylon,
once the foremost city in the whole world.

And located right in the middle of Africa
there is the power named Nubia
where the great lord of Abyssinians rules
and his singular name is Prester John
which comes from Presbyter Iohannes.

Of the New World

And the fourth land
is called Nuevo Mundo
which means the New World
or the new earthe
and it is thus called
because it was detached and diverse
but then discovered.

And this land offered wider ground
to its people from the beginning
but it isn't yet clear
and it hasn't been established
that we are a unity.

This is the largest of the world's parts
and the most advantaged.
Of all the lands here in the world
each of the others
is exceeded by it in size.

Castillo

Huitzilopochtli's Promise

And so Huitzilopochtli answered: "That's good, oh my slave. I will
truly lay out before you the orders of my will and I shall give you
control, with all its precisions. Sustain your hearts on this, follow
my form well. In the end I will take you on—I shall certainly not
abandon you through neglect and I shall surely call to you when the
time comes to move, when we take to the road. Don't feel uneasy,
because I will be with you—I'll not get stuck here. I shall truly con-
sole your heart and it is precisely at this point that I instruct you.
This is the first quality with which you will enhance yourself:
   Eagle & Jaguar; Fire & Water; Arrow & Shield
This will be your indispensable food, this you will live by, so that
you proceed striking terror. The payment for your breast and heart
will be your conquests, your overrunning and destroying the com-
mon people, the dwellers in all the places you reach, and when you
take captives you will cut open their chests with a Flint on the sac-
rificial stone and you will offer their hearts to the brilliant Move-
ment in the sky. And as soon as the heart, rich with blood, is thrust
out, you will offer it in the direction of Huitztlampa, the Thorn Place,

as a sacrificial object, and the blood too, and the bloodiness. And when you have done this I shall be there. Towards Tlaloc also, and then to all my friends, those gods known to you. And you shall eat the flesh unsalted. You may add to it only a little cooked maize, so that it may be eaten.

And the second thing: For those who are special warriors, the brave, the valiant, the impetuous, their name will be The Capturers as I order it and they are the ones who will be without fear for themselves. They will acquire the quilted mantle; the loin-cloth; the painted mantle. Quetzal feathers shall be their insignia; you will go to the source of the feathers and the jade and they shall be given to you and the people will fit you out with them. You will go to those populations who have not known combat, who are unpractised in war and unskilled, those who have settled together on the land, those who have dwelt a long time in one place and where things are flourishing and organized, places in flower, where want has been banished and where everything can be had for the taking by those who work at war.

You will be limited by nothing; nothing will escape you. They will bend to you every wish, whatever your greeds are you will be satisfied, you will take women where and when you please, nothing will escape you, you will receive gifts of everything—the best food, the greatest ease, fragrance, the Flower, tobacco, song, everything, whatever it is."

Tlatelolco Annals

Siege of Tenochtitlan

Auh in yeixquichi ipan mochihua intiquittaque in mahuizoque inte-chocti tetlaocatl inic tlaihiyohuique auh inotlica omitl xaxmantoc tzontli momoyauhtoc calli tzontlapouhtoc calli chichiliuhtoc ocuilti moyacatla otlica auh in caltech chalacatoc in cuatextli auh in atl zayuhqui chichiltic zayuhqui tlapallatl cayuh tiquique tiqui tequix-quiatl auh ocipa tictetzotzomaya xamitl

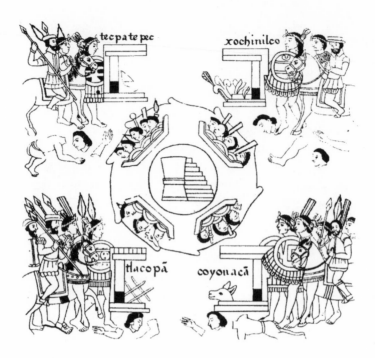

auh iniatlacomoli catoneixcahuil chimaltitla in pieloya inochen aca
mote icequiliznequi zachi maltitla

ticcuaque in tzonpacuahuitl in tequixquizacatl in xantetl in cuetz-
palli quimichi teuhtlaquilli ocuilli

titonetechcuaque in acacelotl inicuac tlepa quimotlaliaya yaycel yey
cuetzin inacayo oncan zan oyhui tleco quicuaya

auh in topatiuh mochiuh in ipatiuh mochiuh telpochtli in tlamacazqui
in ichpochtli in piltzin in ye ixquich macehualli in epatiuh zan ome
matechoctic tlaolli zan matlachtli axaxayacatlaxcalli tequixquiza-
catlaxcalli zan cempoalli topatiuh mochiuh in teocuitlatl in chalchi-
huitl in cuachtli in quetzalli ye ixquich tlazotli atla ipa motlac zan
tetepeuhtoc in ichconquetzque cuauhtematlatl in tianquizco

auh yehuantzin Cuauhtemoctzin quimohuilia in malti amoyuh
quicahua in tecahuato achcauhti tlatlacateca necocquitititza quimititl-
apanaya yoma Cuauhtemoctzin

IMAGES OF THE NEW WORLD

Siege of Tenochtitlan

And all this happened among us. We saw it. We lived through it with
an astonishment worthy of tears and of pity for the pain we suffered.
On the roads lie broken shafts and torn hair;
Houses are roofless, homes are stained red;
Worms swarm in the streets, walls are spattered with brains;
The water is reddish, like dyed water;
We drink it so, we even drink brine;
The water we drink is full of saltpetre;
The wells are crammed with adobe bricks.

Whatever was still alive was kept between shields, like precious trea-
sure, between shields, until it was eaten.

We chewed on hard tzompantli wood, brackish *zacatl* fodder, chunks
of adobe lizards, vermin, dust and worms.

We eat what was on the fire, as soon as it is done we eat it together
right by the fire.

We had a single price; there was a standard price for a youth, a priest,
a boy and a young girl. The maximum price for a slave amounted
to only two handfuls of maize, to only ten tortillas. Only twenty
bundles of brackish fodder was the price of gold, jade, mantles, que-
tzal plumes; all valuables fetched the same low price. It went down
further when the Spaniards set up their battering engine in the mar-
ket place.

Now, Cuauhtemoc orders the prisoners to be brought out; the guards
don't miss any. The elders and chiefs grab them by their extremities
and Cuauhtemoc slits open their bellies with his own hand.

The Aztec Priests' Speech

totecujyoane tlatoquee tlazotitlacae
oanqujmihiyouiltique
ca otlaltitech amacitico
ca njcan amitzinco amocpactzinco
titlachia in timacevalti
ca oamechmaxitilico yn tlacatl totecujo
ca oancomopachiluico
in amatzin amotepetzin
canjn quenamjcan
in oanvalmouicaque
in totecuaca in teteu incha
ca mixtitlan aiauhtitlan
teuatl itic in oammoquixtico
ca amech mixtia amechmonacaztia
amechmotentia in tloque in nauaque
ca njcan iuhqujmma tictlacaitta
njcan tictlacanotza
yn jpalnemoanj
in ioalli in ehecatl
ca ami xiptlava amjpatilloa

ca oticcujque oticanque
yn jhijo in jtlatol in totecujo in tloque navaque
in oanquivalmotquilitiaque
in cemanavac yn tlaltpc tlatoanj in topampa oamechalmjvali
ca njcan ticmaujzoa
ca oanqujvalmotquitilitiaque yn jamux yn jtlacuijlol
in ilhuicac tlatolli in teotlatolli

auh in axcan tlein quenamj
ca tlehuatl in tiqujtozque
in tiqueyazque amonacazpantzinco mach titlatin

The Aztec Priests' Speech

What we say here is for its own reason
beyond response and against our future.

Our revered lords, sirs, dear ones,
take rest from the toil of the road,
you are now in your house and in your nature.
Here we are before you, subjected,
in the mirror of yourselves.
Our sovereign here has let you come,
you have come to rule
as you must in your own place.

Where is it you come from,
how is it that your gods have been scattered
from their municipal centres?
Out of the clouds, out of the mist,
out of ocean's midst you have appeared.
The Omneity takes form in you,
in your eye, in your ear, in your lips.
So, as we stand here,
we see, we address,
the one through whom everything lives,
the night, the Wind,
whose representatives you are.

And we have felt the breath, the word
of our lord the Omneity,
which you have brought with you.
The speaker of the world sent you because of us.
Here we are, amazed by this.
You brought his book with you, his script,
heaven's word, the word of god.

ca zan timacevaltotonti
titlalloque
tizoquiyoque
tivazoque titoxonque
ticocoque titeupouhque
ca zan otech tlaneuj in tlacatl totecujo
inic ipetlanacazco ycpalnacazco
otech motlalili

ca cententli otentli ic tococuepa ic toconjloctia yn
jhiio yn jtlatol in tloque navaque

ic iquatla ytzontia tiqujza
ic tontotlaca in atoiac in tepexic
ic tictemolia ic tiquitlanjlia
in jzomal yn jqualan
ace taqujan ace topoliujan
azo titlatlatziujtique
ieh campa nel nozoc tiazque
ca timacevalti
tipoliujnj timjqujnj
ieh mah ca timjqujcan ieh mah ca tipolihujcan
tel ca teteu in omjcque
ma motlali in amoiollotzin amonacaiotzin

totecujovane
ca achitzin ic tontlaxeloa
in axcan achitzin in tictlapoa
in jtop inijpetlacal
in tlacatl totecujo

anqujmjtalhuja
ca amo tictiximachilia
in tloque navaque in ilhuicava in tlalticpaque
anqujmjtalhuja
ca amo nelli teteu in toteuvan
ca yancuic tlatolli

And now what? How is it,
what are we supposed to say,
what shall we present to your ears?

Can it be said we are anything at all?
We are small subjects.

We are just dirt,
no good,
pressed, reduced to want;
furthermore our sovereign here
mistook us consistently
and has cast us into a corner.

But we refute the logo of the Omneity.

We are down to our skulls in this and we fall over
into the river, into the abyss.
Anger and wrath
will be attracted to our behaviour.
Maybe this is our moment; perhaps this is ruin.

In any case, we shall be dispirited.
Where do we go from here
in our subjection,
reduced, mortalized?
Cut us loose,
because the gods have died.
But you don't have to feel any of this.

Our dear lords,
we share some of it all.
Now we open a little
the store, the treasure casket,
for our sovereign here.

in anqujmjtalhuia
auh ic titotlapolotia ic titotetzauja
ca in totechiuhcava yn oieco yn onemjco tlalticpac
amo iuh qujtotiuj

ca iehoantin techmacatiuj
yn jntlamanjtiliz
iehoantin qujneltocatiuj
quintlaiecultitiuj qujn maviztilitiuj in teteu
iehoantin techmachtitiaque in ixquich
intlaiecoltiloca in immaviztililoca
inic imjxpa titlaqua
inic titizo inic titoxtlava
inic ticopaltema auh inic titlamjctia
quitotiuj ca iehoantin teteu impalnemoa
iehoantin techmaceuhque
injqujn in canjn ynoc iovaya

auh quitotiuj ac iehoantin techmaca
in tococha in toneuhca
auh in ixqujch yn joanj in qualonj
in tonacaiotl in tlaolli in etl in oauhtli in chie
iehoantin tiquimjtlanila
yn atl in qujavitl
inic tlamochiva tlalticpac
no iehoantin mocuiltonoa
motlamachtia
axcavaque iehoantin tlatquiuaque
inic muchipa cemjcac
tlatzmolintoc tlaxoxouixtoc
in inchan in canjn in quenamjca tlaloca
aic tle maianalitztlj vmpa muchiva
atle cocoliztli atle netolinjliztli

auh no iehoa quitemaca
in oquichchotl in tiacauhiotl
in tlamaliztli

You say
that we don't know
the Omneity of heaven and earth.
You say that our gods are not original.
That's news to us
and it drives us crazy.
It's a shock and it's a scandal,
for our ancestors came to earth
and they spoke quite differently.

  They gave us
  their law
  and they believed,
  they served, and they taught the honour among gods;
  they taught the whole service.
  That's why we eat earth before them;
  that's why we draw our blood and do penance;
  and that's why we burn copal and kill the living.
  They were the Lifelord
  and they became our only subject.
  When and where?—In the eldest Darkness.

  They gave us
  our supper and our breakfast,
  all things to drink and eat,
  maize and beans, purslane and sage.
  And we beg them
  for thunder-Rain and Water
  on which the earth thrives.
  They are the rich ones
  and they have more than simply what it takes;
  they are the ones with the stuff,
  all ways and all means, forever,
  the greenness of growth.
  Where and how?—In Tlalocan
  hunger is not their experience
  nor sickness, and not poverty.

auh in tezacatli in tlapiloni
in maxtlatl in tilmatli
in xuchitl in iyetl in chalchiuitl
in quetzalli in teucujtlatl
auh iqujn canjn in ie notzalo in ie tlatlauhtilo
in ie neteuhtilo in ie maujztililo
ca cenca ie vehcauh
yqujn ie tolla yqujn ie vapalcalco
yqujn ie xuchatlappa yqujn ie tlamovanchan
in ie ioalli ychan yqujn ie teutivaca
ca iehoantin novian cemanavac qujtetecatiaque
in jpetl in jmjcpal
iehoantin qujtemaca
in tecuiotl in tlatocaiotl
in tleiotl in maujzzotl
auch cujx ie teoantin toconitlacozq in veve
tlamanjtiliztli
in chichimeca tlamanjtiliztli
in tolteca tlamanjtiliztli
in colhuaca tlamanjtiliztli
in tepaneca tlamanjtiliztli
ca ie iuhca toiolol
ypan ioliva
ypan tlacatiua
ypal nezcatilo ypa nevapavalo
yn jn nonotzaloca in intlatlauhtiloca

huj tetecujoane
ma itla anqujchiualtihtin
in amocuitlapiltzin yn amatlapaltzin
quenoc quilcavaz quenoc qujpoloz
in icnoueue in icmoylama yn jnezcaltiliz
in inevapaualiz
ma techtlaueliti
in teteu
ma intlauel
ma inqualan ypan tiatin

They gave also
the inner manliness, kingly valour
and the acquisitions of the hunt:
the insignia of the lip, the knotting of the mantle,
the loin-cloth, the mantle itself;
Flower and aromatic leaf, jade,
quetzal plumes, and the godshit you call gold.
When and where?—It is a long tradition.
Do you know
when the emplacement of Tula was, of Uapalcalco,
of Xuchatlappan, of Tamoanchan,
of Yoalli ichan, of Teotihuacan?
They were the world-makers who founded
the mat of power, the seat of rule.
They gave
authority and entity,
fame and honour.
And should we now destroy the old law,
the Toltec law,
the Chichimec law,
the Colhua law,
the Tepanec law,
on which the heart of being flows,
from which we animate ourselves,
through which we pass to adulthood,
from which flows our cosmology
and the manner of our prayer?

Oooh! Señores Nuestros,
do nothing;
don't do anything to your population.
It can only bring more ruin,
it can only bring more ruin to the old ones,
our elders, from whom man and woman have grown.

Let us not
anger the gods;

auh ma ic tixco tocpac ieua in cujtlapilli in atlapalli
ma ic ticzoneuhti
ma ic ticacomati
inic tiquilhuja
in aocmo qujnnotzaz in aocmo qujtlatlauhtiz

ma oc yvian yocuxca
xicmottilican totecujyoane in tlein monequj
ca amo vel toiollo pachiuj auh ca za ayamo tontocaquj
ayamo titonelchiua tamechtoiolitlacalvizque
ca njcan onoque
in avaque in tepevaque
in tetecuti in tlatoque
in quitquj in qujmama
in cemanauatl

mazanozoc ye inio yn oticcauhque
in oticpoloque in otoncuililoque
in otocavaltiloque in petlatl in icpalli
ca za oncan tonotiazque za tictzaccutiazque
ma topa xicnochiuilica
in tlein anqujmonequjltizque
ca ixquich ic ticcuepa ic ticnaquilia yn amjhiyotzin
in amotlatoltltzin
totecujyoane

let us not invite their hunger.
Do not unsettle this population.
Why should we agitate them
with what we say amongst ourselves?
If you want peace
don't force the people
to see that we are put aside.

Let's think about this.
At heart, there is no satisfaction for us.
We don't believe, nor do we mock.
We may offend you,
for here stand
the citizens,
the officials,
the chiefs,
the trustees and rulers of this entire world.

It is enough that we have done penance,
that we are ruined,
that we are forbidden and stripped of power.
To remain here is to be imprisoned.
Make of us
the thing that most suits you.
This is all we have to reply,
Señores.

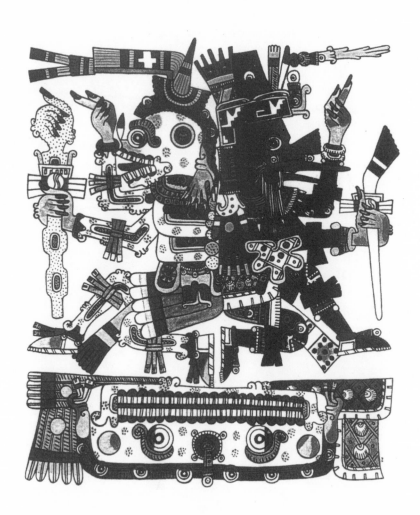

MAYA

Uinal

It was set out this way by the first sage Melchisedek, the first
    Bay tzolci yax ah miatz Merchise yax ah
        prophet, Napuctun, sacerdote, the first priest.
        bovat Napuctun sacerdote yax ah kin
This is the song of how the *uinal* was realized before the world
        was.
    Lay key uchci u zihil uinal ti ma to ahac cab cuchie
He started up from his inherent motion alone.
    ca hoppi u ximbal tuba tu hunal
His mother's mother and her mother, his mother's sister and his
        sister-in-law, they all said:
    Ca yalah u chich ca yalah u dzenaa ca yalah u mim ca yalah u muu
"How shall we say, how shall we see, that man is on the road?"
    bal bin c'alab ca bin c'ilab uinic ti be
These are the words they spoke as they moved along, where there
        was no man.
    cu thanob tamuk u ximbalob cuchie minan uinic cuchi
When they arrived in the east they began to say:
    catun kuchiob te ti likine ca hoppi yalicob
"Who has been here? These are footprints. Get the rhythm of his
        step."
    mac ti mani uay lae he yocob lae ppiz ta uoci
So said the Lady of the world,
    ci bin u than u colel cab
And our Father, Dios, measured his step.
    cabin u ppizah yoc ca yumil ti D[io]s citbil
This is why the count by footstep of the whole world, xoc lah cab
        oc, was called lahca oc 12 Oc.
    lay u chun yalci xoc lah cab oc lae lahca Oc
This was the order born through 13 Oc,
    lay tzolan zihci tumen oxlahun Oc
When the one foot joined its counter-print to make the moment of
        the eastern horizon.

> *uchci u nup tanba yoc likciob te ti likine*

Then he spoke its name when the day had no name,

> *ca yalah u kaba ti minan u kaba kin cuchie*

as he moved along with his mother's mother and her mother, his
mother's sister and his sister-in-law.

> *ximbalnahci y u chiich y u dzenaa y u mim y u muu*

The *uinal* born, the day so named, the sky and earth,

> *zi uinal zihci kin u kaba zihci caan y luum*

the stairway of water, earth, stone and wood, the things of sea and
earth realized.

> *eb haa luum tunich y che zihci u bal kabnab y luum*

1 Monkey, the day he rose to be a day-ity and made the sky and earth.

> *Hun Chuen u hokzici uba tu kuil u mentci caan y luum*

2 Eb he made the first stairway. It ebbed from heaven's heart,

> *Ca Eb u mentci yax eb.   Emci likul tan yol caan*
> the heart of water, before there was earth, stone and wood.
> *tan yol haa, minan luum y tunich y che*

3 Reed, the day for making everything, all there is,

> *Ox Ben u mentci tulacal bal, hibahun bal*
> the things of the air, of the sea, of the earth.
> *u bal caanob y u bal kaknab y u bal luum*

4 Jaguar, he fixed the tilt of the sky and earth.

> *Can Ix uchci u nixpahal caan y luum*

5 Men, he made everything.

> *Ho Men uchci u meyah tulacal*

6 Cib, he made the number-one candle,

> *Uac Cib uchci u mentci yax cib*
> and there was light in the absence of sun and moon.
> *uchci u zazilhal ti minan kin y u*

7 Caban, honey was conceived when we had not a caban.

> *Uuc Caban yax zihci cab ti minan toon cuchi*

8 Flint, his hands and feet were set, he sorted minutiae on the
ground.

> *Uaxac Etznab etzlahci u kab y yoc ca u chichaah yokol luum*

9 Rain, the first deliberation of hell.

> *Bolon Cauac yax tumtabci metnal*

10 Ahau, evil men were assigned to hell out of respect for Dios

*Lahun Ahau uchci u binob u lobil uinicob ti metnal tumen Ds
Citbil*

that they need not be noticed.

ma chicanac cuchie

11 Imix, he construed stone and wood;

Buluc Imix uchci u patic tuni y che

he did this within the face of the day.

lay u mentah ichil kin

12 Wind, occurred the first breath;

Lahcabil Ik uchci u zihzic ik

it was named Ik because there was no death in it.

Lay u chun u kabatic Ik tumen minan cimil ichil lae

13 Night, he poured water on the ground.

Oxlahun Akbal uchci u chaic haa, ca yakzah luum

This he worked into man.

Ca u patah ca uinic-hi

1 Maize, he canned the first anger because of the evil he had
created.

Hunnil Kan u yax mentci u leppel yol tumenel u lobil zihzah

2 Snake, he uncovered the evil he saw within the town.

Ca Chicchan uchci u chictahal u lobil hibal yilah ichil u uich cahe

3 Death, he invented death—

Ox Cimil u tuzci cimil

as it happened the father Ds invented the first death.

uchci u tuzci yax cimil ca yumil ti Ds

———

5 Lamat, he invented the seven great seas.

Ho Lamat lay u tuzci uuclam chac haal kaknab

6 Water, came the deluge and the submersion of everything

Uac Muluc uchci u mucchahal kopob tulacal

before the dawning. Then the father Ds invented the word

*ti mato ahac cabe. Lay uchci yocol u tuz thanil ca yumil ti
Ds*

when there was no word in heaven, when there was neither
stone nor wood.

tulacal ti minan tun than ti caan ti minan tunich y che cuchi

Then the 20 deities came to consider themselves in summation and
    said:
Catun binob u tum tubaob ca yalah tun bayla
"Thirteen units + seven units = one."
Oxlahun tuc: uuc tuc, hun
So said the uinal when the word came in, when there had been no
    word.
Lay yalah ca hok u than ti minan than ti
And this led to the question by the day Ahau, ruler,
Ca katab u chun tumen yax Ahau kin
Why was the meaning of the word not opened to them
ma ix hepahac u nucul than tiob
so that they could declare themselves?
uchebal u thanic ubaobe
Then they went to heaven's heart and joined hands.
Ca binob tan yol caan ca u machaah u kab tuba tanbaobe

Katun 13 Ahau

Katun 2 Ahau ends so that Katun 13 Ahau may be set up. Katun 13 Ahau ends in the sixth *tun* of Katun 9 Ahau: it will keep company with 11 Ahau in the Katun Round. This is its word. Kinchil Coba is the seat of Katun 13 Ahau; and Mayapan. Itzamna, Itzam tzab is its face during it reign.

The ramon nut will be its food. For five *tuns* nuts and fruits will fall from the ramon tree. Three *tuns* will be locust *tuns,* ten generations of them. Bread and water will be unobtainable. The fan shall be displayed, the bouquet shall be displayed, held by Yaxaal Chac in the heavens; Ixma Chucbeni shall arrive to eat sun and moon.

The charge of the katun is doubly heavy. The Batab, impotent and lost, the Ah Kin, impotent and lost, because of Ixma Chucbeni. Perdition of the Halach Uinic, of the Ah Bobat and the Ah Naat; drunkenness of the Ah Bobat and the Ah Kin, because of Ix Dziban Yol Nicte. Derangement through lewdness and adultery begins with the batab, who are corrupt at the start of the reign of Ah Bacocol, who wants devotion and reverence only for himself; the Halach Uinic are scorned in the communities, in the bush and rocky places, by the offspring of the lewd and the perverse, those who despise their elders and forget their maker, the sons of Ah Bacocol. The bread of this katun is not whole because its people are also under Ah Bolon Yocte, those of the two-day mat, the two-day throne, the motherless and the fatherless, the offspring of mad and lewd schemers. The face of the sun and of the moon will be eaten and Balam, the Jaguar, will speak and Ceh, the Deer, will speak, and suffer the stick with groans and make payment to the world by their sudden deaths and their pointless deaths. The charge of sudden and violent deaths will not be over when the great hunger has ceased. This is what the charge of Katun 13 Ahau brings.

Foreigners

They didn't want to join the foreigners
Christianity was not their desire
they didn't want another tax

Those with their sign in the bird
those with their sign in the stone, flat worked stone
5   those with their sign in the jaguar—three emblems—:
four times four hundred *hab* was the period of their lives
plus fifteen score *hab* before that period ended
because they knew the rhythm of the days in themselves.

10   Whole the moon whole the *hab*
whole the day whole the night
whole the breath when it moved too whole the blood too
when they came to their beds their mats their thrones;
rhythm in their reading of the good hours
15   rhythm in their search for the good days
as they observed the good stars enter their reign
as they watched the reign of the good stars begin
Everything was good.

For they kept sound reason
20   there was no sin in the holy faith of their lives
there was no sickness they had no aching bones
they had no high fever they had no smallpox
they had no burning chest they had no bellyache
they had no chest disease they had no headache
25   The course of mankind was ciphered clearly.
Not what the foreigners arranged when they came here
Then shame and terror were preferred
carnal sophistication in the flowers of Nacxit Xuchit and his
    circle
no more good days were shown to us
30   this was the start of the two-day chair, the two-day rule
this was the start of our sickness also

there were no good days for us, no more sound reason.
At the end of the loss of our vision and of our shame
    everything will be revealed.
There was no great priest no lord speaker no lord priest
35 with the change of rulers when the foreigners came
The priests they set down here were lewd
they left their sons here at Mayapan
These in turn received their affliction from the foreigners called
    the Itza.
The saying is: since foreigners came three times
40 three score *hab* is the age to get us exempted from tax
The trouble was the aggression of those men the Itza
we didn't do it we pay for it today
But there is an agreement at last to make us and the foreigners
    unanimous
Failing that we have no alternative to war

Christian Justice

... the true God, the true *Dios,* came, but this was the origin too of affliction for us. The origin of tax, of our giving them alms, of trial through the grabbing of petty cacao money, of trial by blowgun, stomping the people, violent removal, forced debt, debt created by false testimony, petty litigation, harassment, violent removal, the collaboration with the Spaniards on the part of the priests, the local chiefs, the choirmasters, public prosecutors through the agency of the children and the youths of the town, and all the while the mistreated were further maltreated. These were the people who had been reduced to want but who did not depart even when they were so squeezed. It was through Antichrist on earth, the kinkajous of the towns, the vixen of the towns, blood-sucking bugs of the town, those who suck dry the common people. But it will happen that tears will come to the eyes of God the father. The *justicia* of God the father will settle on the whole world, it surely will come from God upon Ah Kantenal, Ix Pucyola, the opportunists of the world.

Finis

10   Yok tuba in than,
11   cen Chilam Balam, ca in tzolah u than
12   hahal Ku tuzinile yokol cabe; yubi
13   hunac tzuc ti cabe, yume, u than Dios, u Yumil
14   caan y luum. Hach utz ka u than ti caan,
15   yume, Cokol yahaulil, yokol ix ca pixan/
16   hahal Ku. Heuac heob ti ulez lae, yume, ox al a mukil
17   <i>x cuch lum idzinil. Dzaman yol, cimen ix u puc-
18   zikal tu nicteob xan, ah uaua tulupoob, ah ua
19   tan zinaob, Nacxit Xuchit tu nicte u lakob,
20   ca-ca-kin yahaulilob, coylac te tu dzamob,
1   coylac te tu nicteob. Ca-ca kin uinicil u than-
2   [n]ob. Ca-ca-kin u xecob, u luchob, u ppoocob,
3   u co kin[n]ob, u co akab, u maxilob yokol
4   cab. Kuy cu cal, mudz cu uich, pudz cu chi,
5   ti yahaulil cabob, yume. He, cu talel minan
6   hah tu thanob u dzulilob cah. Bin yalob
7   hach talanilob, u mehen Uuc-tocoy-naob,
8   yalob Uuc-tocoy-naobe, yume.
                                    Mac to ah
9   bovat, mac to ah kin bin tohol cantic
10   u than uooh lae?
                        Finis.

Finis

10   This alone is the word
11   I, Chilam Balam, have interpreted the word
12   of the true god of all places in the world
13   in every part of the world it is heard, oh father
14   of sky and earth. Splendid indeed is his word in heaven
15   oh father, his rule over us, over our souls.
16   Yet as thrice the offspring of animals are the old men

17 of the younger brothers of the land. Snarled minds, hearts
   dead
18 in carnal sophistication, who too often turn back, who
19 propagate Nacxit Xuchit through the sophistication of his
   circle
20 the two-day rulers, lustful on their thrones
1 lustful in their sophistication. Two-day men, their words
2 two-day their seats, their bowls, their hats
3 the day crime, the night crime, hoods of the world.
4 They turn back their necks, they wink their eyes, they
   drool

                                              at the mouth
5 before our own representatives, oh father. See,
6 when they come the foreigners bring no truth.
7 Yet great secrets are told by the sons of men
8 and the women of seven ruined houses

                                  Who is the prophet
9 who is the priest who shall read
10 the word of this book
                      Finis

Ritual of the Bacabs

Healing Song

This is to cool burning fever and to cool fire, the ailment fire.

My foot's coolness, my hand's coolness,
    as I cooled this fire.
Fivefold my white hail, my black hail, yellow hail,
    as I cool the fire.
Thirteenfold my red cloth, my white cloth, black cloth,
yellow cloth,
    when I answered the strength of this fire.
A black fan my emblem,
    as I answered the strength of this fire.
With me comes the white water-maize,
    and I answered the strength of this fire.
With me comes the white water-lily,
    and I have answered the strength of this fire.
Just now I settled my foot's coolness, my hand's coolness.
    Amen.

Nakuk Pech

I built my House

When the foreigners came to the towns of this land, there were no
Maya men who wanted to pay tax to the first of them to arrive.
Hence these first Spaniards made an account of those towns which
were to be given to be governed. I, Nakuk Pech, was the first recip-
ient of this town in the district Chac Xulub Chen.

In the year 1552 the padres settled here. In this year they came to
teach singing here at Sisal. They came from the west to teach the

chants of mass and vespers, to the music of the organ and flute, and plainsong, which we had not known here before.

In the year 1553 the Auditor Don Tomás López arrived in this land of Yucatan from Castile, as a messenger from the great ruler Rey de Castilla to protect us from the hand of the Spaniards here. He put an end to burning by the Spaniards, an end to savaging by mastiffs, he originated the appointing of chiefs in the towns, by the gift of the yardstick; he also adjusted the rate of tax. Three times we paid tribute to the Spaniards: blankets, beeswax, turkeys, maize, wooden buckets, salt, peppers, broad beans, narrow beans, jars, pots, vases—a list of the tribute payable to the *encomendero* before the auditor turned his attention to these matters.

So too I built my house of stone on the north side of the church. To prevent Maya men saying it belongs to them, this is why I set out what was done by me, Don Pablo Pech Ah Macan Pech, my father, Don Martín Pech Ah Kon Pech, and my lord Don Ambrosio Pech whose Maya name is Op Pech, and Ixil Ytzam Pech, and Don Esteban Pech Ah Culub Pech.

Paxbolon

Death of Cuauhtemoc

Cuauhtemoc, the emperor who had come from Mexico-Tenochtitlan with Cortés, was there. He said to Paxbolonacha, the ruler I mentioned earlier: "My lord, as for these Spaniards, the day will come when they will cause you much trouble and kill your people. I believe rather we should kill them, for I bring a large force and you are many." So spoke Cuauhtemoc to Paxbolonacha, ruler of the Mactun. On hearing these words of Cuauhtemoc, the other replied that he would first have to think it over. He considered that the word of the Spaniards was good; they did not kill or abuse people. They only asked for much honey, turkeys, maize and fruit, every day. He said to himself: "I will not be equivocal or double-hearted towards the Spaniards." Not so Cuauhtemoc, the Mexican leader, who wanted to kill the Spaniards, and urged him on. In view of this, Paxbolonacha went to Cortés: "My lord Capitán del Valle, this ruler Cuauhtemoc who is with you, watch out for him in case he commits treason against you; three, four times he has told me you should be killed." Cortés heard this. Immediately the Mexican was seized and put in chains. On the third day that he was a prisoner they took him out and baptized him, whether with the name Don Juan or with the name Don Fernando is unsure. He received a name and was sliced through the neck. His head was hung in the ceiba tree before the sanctuary in Yaxdzan.

QUECHUA

Thunder

Fair princess,
your brother has broken your jar
that is why
it thunders and lightens

so princess
you give us falling rain
or else hail and snow

Viracocha
earth-establisher, earth maker
for this duty
has established you, has made you

Dawn

Viracocha, you say
may the sun be, may the night be
you say
may it dawn, may it grow light
you make your son to move in peace, in safety
to give light and illumination to the people
you have created oh Viracocha:

peacefully, safely
sun, shine on and illumine
the Incas, the people, the servants
whom you have shepherded
guard them from sickness and suffering
in peace, in safety

Potatoes, Maize

Oh Viracocha, ancient Viracocha,
skilled creator,
who makes and establishes,
"on the earth below
may they eat
may they drink"
you say;
for whose you have established
those you have made
may food be plentiful.

"Potatoes, maize,
all kinds of food
may there be"
you say, who command and
       increase;
so then they shall not suffer,
and not suffering, do you will;
may there be no frost, no hail,
keep them in peace.

Eclipse

How the sun died.

Long ago the sun is said to have died.
For five days after its death it was night.
The stones began to jostle each other;
the mortars, large and small, began to eat people,
the pestles too.
The mountain llamas attacked people.
As Christians we account for this today
by saying that it was the eclipse at Jesus Christ's
death. And possibly it was.

Viracocha & child

In the ancient past, this god Cuniraya Viracocha walked and travelled as a man, making himself look like a pauper, with his mantle and shirt torn. Those who didn't know him called after him: "Flea-ridden wretch!" Now this man founded all the towns here. By his word alone he created fields and terraces with their solid retaining walls. He taught irrigation and opened the canals by dropping the bloom of the pupunha. And thereafter he traveled around, doing this and that, and conquered other, local, gods in his wisdom.

At this time lived a woman, also a god, called Cavillaca. This Cavillaca was still a virgin, though very beautiful, so that her fellow gods were always thinking how to bed her. She said yes to none of them.

One day this woman whom no man had ever touched sat down by herself to weave at the foot of a lucuma tree. In his wisdom, Coniraya Viracocha perched on this tree as a bird. Then he put his seed into a ripe lucuma fruit and let it fall near the woman. She ate it avidly. In this fashion she became pregnant, without actually knowing a man. In the ninth month she gave birth; she breast-fed the child for a year, asking herself: "Whose son is this?"

When the child was a year old and could crawl, she summoned her fellow gods, to discover who the father was. On receiving the summons, the other gods were much pleased. They all put on their best clothes and arrived thinking: "Maybe I'll be the lucky one." The gathering was held in Anchicocha, where the woman lived. After all the gods had sat down in a row, the woman said: "See, good men and lords, look at this child. Who among you engendered him in me? You, or you …?" and she asked each of them, and no one said: "I did."

Now since Coniraya Viracocha had sat himself right at the end of the row and looked really wretched, she didn't ask him in her disgust, thinking: "How could the child be the son of this beggar?" for the rest were finely dressed.

As no one said: "He's my son," she said to the boy: "Go and find your father yourself," and she warned the gods: "If one of you is his father, he'll try to climb up on to you." The boy began crawling along and ignored everyone until he came right to the other end of the row where his father sat. At this point he chuckled and crawled up onto his father's lap.

However, when the mother saw this she exclaimed angrily: "Have I borne so wretched a son!" and picking the child up went off towards the sea. Reckoning she would love him for it, Coniraya Viracocha put his golden suit on and, while the local gods trembled, pursued her. He stood up and cried: "Sister Cavillaca, come back, please; look at me, I'm quite handsome now."

At which he illuminated the earth.

Invasion

The Inca ordered that thirty men from Upper and Lower Yauyos should serve the god Pariacaca in the month of Pura. And fifteen men from each district served the god, giving him food. One day they sacrificed one of their llamas, whose name was Yauri Huanaca.

As the thirty priests gathered to examine the llama's heart and entrails, one of their number, Llacuas Quita Pariasca, said:

"This is not a good moment, brothers. Before long our father Pariacaca will regress into the past age of the Purun."

But the others said: "That's only your opinion," and one went on: "Why do you say that? Through this heart our father Pariacaca speaks good." He didn't go near the heart, but still pronounced: "Pariacaca himself says so, brother." And they insulted Llacuas Quita Pariasca, saying angrily: "The stinker, what does he know! Our father Pariacaca's realm stretches through the Chinchasuyu, how could he be superseded! What does this man know?"

A few days later they all heard the news: the Spaniards were in Caxamarca [Cajamarca].

Moreover, among the thirty priests was an old man from Checa (*ayllu* Cacasica) who was the wisest of them all; he was called Caxalliuya. When the Spaniards reached here they asked: "Where is the silver belonging to this god, and his regalia?" Since none of the priests wanted to say, the Spaniards grew furious; they heaped up some grass and put Caxalliuya to burn. The wind whipped the flames up one side of his body and he suffered terribly. Only then were the silver and regalia given to the Spaniards. All the priests agreed:

"Llacuas Quita Pariasca gave us good advice, brothers. It's best we disperse; this is not a good moment."

And each went off to his community.

Guaman Poma

Love Song

mana soncoyqui queuiccho
mana uacaycunyacuy
cicllallay caspa
coyallay caspa
ñustallay caspa
uniyuiquellan apariuan
yucuy parallan pusaiuan
chay llicllayquita ricuycuspa
chay acsoyquita camaycuspa
mananam pachapas chiciancho
tuta ricchariptipas
mana tacmi pacha
pacarincho
camca coya, camca senora
mananachi yuyariaunquicho
cay zancaypi poma atoc
micouaptin
cay pinaspi
uichicasca quicasca tiapti palla

Love Song

doesn't your heart hurt
don't you want to cry
you, my precious flower
you, my queen,
you, my princess
see how justice takes me off in
    spate
and imprisons me
when I glimpse your mantle
when I see your dress
the day does not exist for me
in this night I awake to know
it will never dawn;
I think that you,
my queen, my señora,
don't remember me
I'm eaten up
by the puma and the fox of the
    zancay
I'm alone,
disheartened and lost, my lady.

Cochabamba Song

Carnival

Carnavalmá kasqa,
uj machitu kasqa.
Chaka uramanta
wataqamusqasqa
ñóqay rikurqoni
such'i barbas kasqa;
alforjasninpipis
ískay runtus kasqa;
upirísaj nini,
meq'arájtaj kasqa.

Carnival

The carnival was
a sad old man it was
under the bridge
sniffing around he was
I saw him with his
such'i fish moustache
in his bag
two eggs there were
I tried to grab them
but hollow they were

José María Arguedas

_____

Wayanaysi

Wayanaysi rapran
manaya k'an hinachu,
mak'ta, runa.

K'ollk'e chalwas *ahujan*

mapu k'ochapi
manaya k'an hinachu
mak'ta, runa.

Swallow

The swallow moves its wings
not so fast as you
boy, man.

The silver fish moves through
        the waters
of river and lake
not so fast as you
boy, man.

OTHER NATIVE
AMERICAN LANGUAGES

Huitoto

Genesis

naino mikade inyede nainona
fore hetaide momade
hana hetaide dyidde mikade
moma Nainuema nikaido abi mosinyote
      abina
               henorite
mika amena inyede mosinyote
nainokoni nikai igaido mosinyote
                   hafaikido
ninomo hinade naino ihiyake fakaode
fakademo dyiide hinade dyireike
                fakade dyidde
habi henode momade bikino hidyake fakade

hinade naino hidyake medyeridode
      nikai igaido dyirireidode
momade hinade arebaike nitanode
           arebaike nikariode
      iseikedo mosinyote
naino hidyake naino gaitanode
      nitade nitade
      gaitanode mosinyote gaitaikeda
iesa rainadate inikoni nikaranikoni
      inidyomoreidade
naino mosinyote
muitade imugi ie fue imugu imuguri muitade
naino mosinyokeda
iesa rainadate birunyukoni
ie biko hirenote birunyu gaiktaikeda
      hirenote biko mogoguito koreko
         ie henikekoni iesaai abina
            henohenorite
bikino komuitate
kai ari atidiekino Rafuema

Genesis

a phantasma, *naino,* nothing else
the father touched the image of the phantasm
        touched a secret, nothing else
the father Nainu-ema, who-has-the-phantasm, held it by a dream
to himself
          thought hard about it
he held nothing substantial
he held the phantasma by the thread of a dream
          by the line of his breath
in the void he probed for the mass of the phantasma
the probe was nothing: "I fasten on the void"
          he probed nothing
Then the father thought hard and probed for the mass of the word-
   thing
in the void he fastened on to the mass of the phantasma with the
   thread of a dream
in the void the father pressed his adhesive
   dreamed his adhesive on to it
   held it by the thinnest thread
he seized the mass of the phantasma
   pressed and pressed it
   seized, held and seized it again
then he set himself on the plain, this dream earth
   stepped on to the plain
he held the phantasma
he spat spittle from his mouth he spat again and again
he held the phantasma firm
then he set himself on this earthly part
he peeled off the sky, he seized the earth
   peeled off the blue sky and the white sky
       At the base of the sky, Rafu-ema, who-has-the-story,
                       thought hard about it
let these words be made
here above we relate them

Guarani

Ñamandu

The true father Ñamandu, the First One,
     from a minimum of his spirit,
     from the knowledge in his spirit,
     having his engendering knowledge,
made the flames, the mists arise.

Having stood,
     from the knowledge in his spirit,
     having his engendering knowledge,
he himself conceived the origin of future speech;
     from the knowledge in his spirit,
     having his engendering knowledge,
our father fostered the origin of speech, made it of his spirit;
     when the earth was not
     in the heart of the eldest darkness
     when knowledge was not,
the true father Ñamandu, the First One,
     fostered the origin of future speech, made it of his spirit.

Having himself conceived the origin of future speech,
     from the knowledge of his spirit,
     having his engendering knowledge,
he himself conceived the origin of future love;
     when the earth was not,
     in the heart of the eldest darkness,
     when knowledge was not,
     having his engendering knowledge,
he himself conceived the origin of future love.

Having fostered the origin of future speech,
having fostered a minimum of love,
     from the knowledge in his spirit,
     having his engendering knowledge,

he fostered the origin of a minimal chant;
    when the earth was not,
    in the heart of the eldest darkness,
    when the knowledge was not,
he himself fostered a minimal chant.

Having himself fostered the origin of future speech,
having himself fostered a minimum of love,
having himself fostered a minimal chant,
    he prospected who
        should share the origin of speech,
        should share the minimum of love,
        should share the thread of the chant;
having prospected,
    from the knowledge in his spirit,
    having his engendering knowledge,
he fostered the future companions of his spirit.

Having prospected,
    from the knowledge in his spirit,
    having his engendering knowledge,
he fostered the big-hearted Ñamandu
he fostered them equally with the brilliance of his knowledge,
    when the earth was not,
    in the heart of the eldest darkness;
he fostered the big-hearted Ñamandu
    as the true fathers of many future sons,
    as the true fathers of the logos of many future sons,
he fostered the big-hearted Ñamandu.

In addition,
    from the knowledge in his spirit,
    having his engendering knowledge,
with the true father of the future Karai
with the true father of the future Jakaira
with the true father of the future Tupa
he shared the knowledge of his spirit;

as the true fathers of many future sons,
of the logos of many future sons,
he shared with them the knowledge of his spirit.

In addition,
the true father Ñamandu,
to reciprocate his heart,
shared the knowledge of his spirit
with the future true mother Ñamandu;
the true father Karai
shared the knowledge of his spirit
to reciprocate his heart
with the future mother Karai.

The true father Jakaira, likewise,
to reciprocate his heart,
shared the knowledge of his spirit
with the future mother Jakaira.

The true father Tupa, likewise,
to reciprocate his heart,
shared the knowledge of his spirit
with the future mother Tupa.

They having shared in the knowledge of the spirit of the First One
in the origin of future speech,
in the origin of love,
in the thread of the chant.
they joined together in the origin of his engendering knowledge.

So we call them too
the excellent true fathers of the logos,
the excellent true mothers of the logos.

Curing Song

ωτ	rapidly you have come here, kingfisher, you white one
t	you are magical
t	you never fail
t	high above, resting there
t	rapidly you are descending
t	the disease you have come to take away with you
t	a second time you never appear

ωτ = s-ge or "ske," the formal opening of the chant

t = ha, a noise of stress and encouragement.

Ketigisti Thomson, Notebook

W. W. Long, Notebook

Cakchiquel Maya

Suffering

On the day 13 Reed [12 August 1530] ended the thirty-fourth "year" *[huna]* after the revolution.

During this year heavy tribute was imposed. Gold was contributed to Tunatiuh; four hundred men and four hundred women were contributed to work in Pangan on the construction of the city, by order of Tunatiuh. All this, all, we ourselves saw, oh, my sons!

On the day 10 Reed [16 September 1531] ended the thirty-fifth "year" *[huna]* after the revolution.

During the two months of the third year which had passed since the lords presented themselves, the king 9-Maize died; he died on the day 7 Deer [24 September 1532] while he was panning gold. Immediately after the death of the king, Tunatiuh came here to choose a successor to the king. Then the lord *Don Jorge* was installed in the government by order of Tunatiuh alone. There was no election by the people to name him. Afterwards Tunatiuh talked to the lords and his orders were obeyed by the chiefs, for in truth they feared Tunatiuh.

Otomi

Lament

gumbgue na tzitzo
   tzu teranetzi
nugua tzimajay
   matzi nadunthi danvuigui
tzagueto narantzivi natzi

             narancuay

   dijequi dithiegmi
narandohi

di tzirajahy
nestihi napehde
   nadeni nuarabuiy
nubui tziudi
   tiumbi nua rantzu
nubui istindee
   ytzoni nadu aranbuiy
gato nua namethi najay
   da huadi
nua na nestihi nanbuigui
   dibgetze na octzi
gato na tzandi najay
   nanigee
otho tevea
   da pay unime
ogui
   agui
ytzege ya dothte
   ya ne ya puethe
ajonto
   tambengui

Lament

the willow stands erect
   so pride flourishes
here in the world
   it may live long
but the fire-axe

   splits it
the Wind
   throws it down
ephemeral is the count
   of Flower life

at sunrise
  it burgeons
at sunset
  it weeps in death
the whole thing on earth
  must end
life is ephemeral
  and sinks into the pit
the whole earth belly
  is a grave
there is nothing
  it can sustain
it hides
  it buries
the water course, the river
  the stream, the spring:
none
  goes back

Endnotes to *Images of the New World*

From *Image of the New World. The American Continent portrayed in Native Texts* (Thames & Hudson: London & New York, 1979); "The Suns" first appears in this volume. The orthography of the native-language texts in general follows that of the sources from which they are taken, although some spellings have been standardized in the interests of legibility.

Nahuatl

4. Cuauhtitlan Annals: a 16th-century manuscript in part transcribed from pre-Cortesian annals *(xiuhmolpilli);* together with the Legend of the Suns it is sometimes referred to under the joint title *Codex Chimalpupoca* (also *History of the Kingdoms of Mexico and Colhuacan).*

7. illustration: Aztec Sunstone.

13. illustration: Laud Codex, p.45.

17. Cantares mexicanos: a collection of poems and songs originally composed and performed at the Aztec court in Tenochtitlan (today, Mexico City), at which Nezahualcoyotl, the "poet-king" of Texcoco (1402–72), was prominent.

24. Chimalpahin: San Anton Muñón Chimalpahin Cuauhtlehuanitzin (1579-ca. 1660), a major Nahuatl historian who, like Cristóbal del Castillo (1526–1606), using the pre-Cortesian books of Mexico as his sources, was led to question the universal validity of Biblical and western history.

25. "The Four Continents": adapted and translated into Nahuatl by Chimalpahin from Enrico Martínez's *Reportorio de los tiempos y historia natural desta Nueva España* (Mexico 1606).

32. illustration: Tlaxcala Lienzo.

34. Aztec Priest's Speech: delivered in response to the missioneering efforts made by the 12 Franciscan friars sent to Mexico in 1524 by Pope Hadrian and the Emperor Charles V; later recorded by Bernardino de Sahagún, who also compiled the Florentine Codex.

43. illustration: Mexican symbols of wealth and power.

Maya

44. illustration: "Quetzalcoatl and Mictlantecutli," Borgia Codex, p. 56.

46. Chilam Balam: the collective name of histories, in part transcribed from hieroglyphic originals, written and kept in the towns of Yucatan, among them Chumayel.

46. "uinal": a calendar period of twenty days, each named by one of the Twenty Signs of Mesoamerican ritual which here are combined successively with the Thirteen Numbers.

55. illustration: Last page of Chilam Balam Book of Chumayel.

56. Nakuk Pech: author of the Chronicle of Chac-Xulub-Pech; collaborated with the Spaniards.

Quechua

61/65. illustration: From Guaman Poma's *Nueva corónica*.

62. Huarochiri Narrative: Quechua manuscript of the early 17th century; also known under such titles as *Runa yndio, Dioses y hombres de Huarochirí* and *Los hijos de Pariacaca*.

66. Guaman Poma: the author of the *Nueva corónica*, written between 1587 and 1613 and sent as a letter to Philip III of Spain; this is the source of the "love song," and of the accompanying line drawings.

69. José María Arguedas: author of the novel *Los rios profundos* (1958), in which "Swallow" appears.

Other languages

74. Ñamandu: from the major Guarani cosmogony *Ayvu Rapyta*.

77. illustration: Cherokee syllabary.

78. Lament: customarily attributed to Nezahualcoyotl (see above), whose mother tongue was Otomi.

78. "Tunatiuh" means "sun" in Nahuatl; name given to Pedro Alvarado on account of his fair hair.

PALABRA DE GUERRILLERO

POESIA GUERRILLERA
DE LATINOAMERICA

Ernesto Che Guevara

Canto a Fidel

Vámonos
ardiente profeta de la aurora,
por recónditos senderos inalámbricos
a liberar el verde caimán que tanto amas.

Vámonos
derrotando afrentas con la frente
plena de martianas estrellas insurrectas,
juremos lograr el triunfo o encontrar la muerte.

Cuando suene el primer disparo y se despierte
en virginal asombro la manigua entera,
allí, a tu lado, serenos combatientes,
nos tendrás.

Cuando tu voz derrame hacia los cuatro vientos
reforma agraria, justicia, pan, libertad,
allí, a tu lado, con idénticos acentos,
nos tendrás.

Y cuando llegue al final de la jornada
la sanitaria operación contra el tirano,
allí, a tu lado, aguardando la postrer batalla,
nos tendrás.

El día que la fiera se lama el flanco herido
donde el dardo nacionalizador le dé,
allí, a tu lado, con el corazón altivo,
nos tendrás.

No pienses que puedan menguar nuestra entereza
las decoradas pulgas armadas de regalos;
pedimos su fusil, sus balas y una peña.
Nada más.

Ernesto Che Guevara

Song to Fidel

You said the sun would rise.
Let's go
along those unmapped paths
to free the green alligator you love.

And let's go obliterating
insults with our
brows swept with dark insurgent stars.
We shall have victory or shoot past death.

At the first shot the whole jungle
will awake with fresh amazement and
there and then serene company
we'll be at your side.

When your voice quarters the four winds
reforma agraria, justice, bread, freedom,
we'll be there with identical accents
at your side.

And when the clean operation against the tyrant
ends at the end of the day
there and then set for the final battle
we'll be at your side.

And when the wild beast licks his wounded side
where the dart of Cuba hits him
we'll be at your side
with proud hearts.

Don't ever think our integrity can be sapped
by those decorated fleas hopping with gifts
we want their rifles, their bullets and a rock
nothing else.

Y si en nuestro camino se interpone el hierro,
pedimos un sudario de cubanas lágrimas
para que se cubran los guerrilleros huesos
en el tránsito a la historia americana.
Nada más.

México, año 1956

Anonymous

_____

¡Prosigan guerrilleros!

Ha muerto Luis Felipe de la Puente
esperanza de mil pueblos explotados,
aquel que en una lucha sin cuartel,
acercándose al peligro frente a frente,
dejó su sangre y corazón regados.

Pero él prendió ese fuego inapagable,
que ilumina nuestra gran revolución,
y a los gritos de: ¡mueran los cobardes!
sin temor de nada ni de nadie,
continuaremos su brillante acción.

¡Prosigan Guerrilleros!
continuen la grandiosa empresa
que la Historia les impuso en nuestro suelo.
Que se oiga la viril protesta,
al fúnebre compás de las ráfagas de fuego.

¡Prosigan Guerrilleros!
Os lo piden nuestros pueblos oprimidos
ya es hora de que acaben para siempre
la injusticia, el hambre, la miseria,
el dolor, la angustia, los gemidos …

And if iron stands in our way
we ask for a sheet of Cuban tears
to cover our guerrilla bones
on the journey to American history.
Nothing more.

Anonymous

Forward Guerrillas!

Luis Felipe de la Puente
hope of a thousand assaulted peoples
has died in the relentless maws
turning his final face toward danger
his blood his heart dredged with cause.

But he fired this brilliant torch
hostile light of our revolution
and kindled the shout Let cowards die!
inside no fear of anything or body
we shall make good that cry.

Forward Guerrillas!
Carry on the vast construction
history left half built on our soil
let our male anger beat in their ears
to the funereal roll and flash of fire.

Forward Guerrillas!
Now is the time amigos
injustice poverty pain
anguish and groaning be closed
and in themselves for ever slain.

Ya nada los detiene hermanos nuestros,
están desesperados los impíos,
saben que al amanecer de un nuevo día
nuestros serán los campos y las flores,
el viento, los pájaros, los ríos …

Entonces flameará nuestra bandera
otra luz alumbrará nuestros caminos
se acabará el hambre, la miseria
aquella explotación vil y miserable,
que tanto tiempo callados padecimos.

¡Prosigan Guerrilleros!
Son suyos los laureles de la gloria,
nos lo dirá el paso de los años venideros,
y el transcurso inexorable de la historia

¡Prosigan valientes y aguerridos guerrilleros!

Luis Nieto

Canción para los héroes del pueblo

Venid a ver a los hombres
que mataron los soldados,
parece que aún sonríen
a la Libertad sus labios.

Venid a ver a los pobres
muertos de veinte balazos.
Hasta los mismos fusiles
les admiraban sonámbulos.

Nothing holds us back now
the godless are desperate
they know across the hour of the New
the fields the flowers the wind
the sierras the rivers will be ours.

Then our thing will fly
another light will light our street
no more hunger and poverty
that miserable and ugly trick
we let happen in the past.

Forward Guerrillas!
You are the full sails of glory
the passage of years to come
and the hard beat of history
has to tell us that

Onward valiant and warborn guerrillas!

Luis Nieto

Song

Now look at the men
struck dead by the hired guns
their parted lips seem still
to be smiling at freedom

Come now and see
those poor men shot
by twenty guns whose barrels
looked on shocked and somnambulant

Amaban la Libertad
tal como la aman los bravos
para matarlos fue urgente
lo hicieran a cañonazos.

¡Venid a ver a los héroes!
¡Venid a verlos, hermanos!
Están aquí con sus pechos
de sangre condecorados.

Que formen guardia de guerra
brigadas de milicianos
y que sus tumbas vigilen
los volcanes milenarios.

Y en vez que cubran sus cuerpos
tristes banderas de llanto,
hagámosles un incendio
de himnos revolucionarios.

¡No han muerto! Contra los nuestros
nada pueden los disparos.
En el corazón del pueblo
ellos vivirán mil años.

¡Y ahora nada de lágrimas!
¡Puños y pechos blindados!
¡Y a pelear como leones
porque ellos no han muerto en vano!

They fell in with freedom
as laughing men to love her
And only the remote guess
of cannon shot could strike them down

Turn your eyes on the heroes
Come and see them brothers!
There they are their chests cool
with the black decor of blood

Make the horizon sound of brigades
make a band of war
and may the everlasting volcanos
stand guard over their graves

Let us not cover their bodies
with the beaten flags of weeping
make for them a fire wreath
of rising songs to ring their spirits

They have not died, against our men
those bullets can do nothing
theirs is the pulse stars have
in the hearts of the people

So no talk of tears now
with closed hands and armed chests
turn and circle like lions
because these dead turn within us

Javier Heraud

Palabra de guerrillero

Porque mi Patria es hermosa
como una espada en el aire
y más grande ahora y aún
y más hermosa todavía,
yo hablo y la defiendo
con mi vida.
No me importa lo que digan
los traidores
hemos cerrado el paso
con gruesas lágrimas
de acero.
El cielo es nuestro.
Nuestro el pan de cada día,
hemos sembrado y cosechado
el trigo y la tierra,
son nuestros
y para siempre nos
pertenecen
el mar,
las montañas
y los pájaros.

Arte poética

En verdad, en verdad hablando,
la poesía es un trabajo difícil
que se pierde o se gana
al compás de los años otoñales.

Javier Heraud

I Give You My Word

My country is beautiful
a sword thrust in the air
and greater now
               and still
and yet more
               beautiful.
               And so
I speak and defend it
with my life.
What the traitors say
can't touch me.
We have stood in their way
with tears
of steel.
Heaven is ours
we have made
our daily bread
harvested the grain
this earth: our spirit
and for ever
the sea
the sierras
the birds.

Ars Poetica

It is true
poetry is close work
the pattern is made or lost
in a rhythm of autumnal years, no turning back.

(Cuando uno es joven
y las flores que caen no se recogen
uno escribe y escribe entre las noches,
y a veces se llenan cientos y cientos
de cuartillas inservibles.
Uno puede alardear y decir
"yo escribo y no corrijo,
los poemas salen de mi mano
como la primavera que derrumbaron
los viejos cipreses de mi calle")
Pero conforme pasa el tiempo
y los años se filtran entre las sienes,
la poesía se va haciendo
trabajo de alfarero,
arcilla que se cuece entre las manos,
arcilla que moldean fuegos rápidos.

Y la poesía es
un relámpago maravilloso,
una lluvia de palabras silenciosas,
un bosque de latidos y esperanzas,
el canto de los pueblos oprimidos,
el nuevo canto de los pueblos liberados.

Y la poesía es entonces,
el amor, la muerte,
la redención del hombre.

Madrid, 1961   La Habana, 1962

(I am young . . .
some of the fallen flowers are not picked up
I write on and on through the avenues of night
and sometimes hundreds of useless
sheets of paper are covered.
I say, in the fire of pride
"I write and make no corrections
poems come from my hand
and are destroyed as springtime always is
by the old cypresses in my street")

But time flows
as measured years between my temples
and the utterance turns,
shaped while glistening clay
between the hands
and baked by those quick fires.

The thing is marvellous
              lightning
                        rain
              of silent words
a rain forest in the heart gets
the unending drift of hope
the long song of saddened peoples
the quick new song of the liberated

it is love then and death
and our way clear.

Las moscas

Claro, señorita mosca,
Ud. vuela graciosamente
Ud. se dibuja en el aire,
se dibuja con su sombra
movediza en las paredes,
Ud. parece reirse de mí,
porque yo ni la miro
débilmente,
y Ud. se posa en mi nariz,
se para en mi cabeza,
se posa sobre mi hombro
y hasta diría le gusta,
ay señorita mosca,
que yo le ponga
inútilmente mi mano
para matarla,
pues Ud. se ahuyenta,
levanta el vuelo,
y se posa sobre mi pan,
mis tostadas, mis libros
que aguardan su llegada.
¡Ay! señorita mosca,
me dicen que Ud. puede
traer males terribles,
pero yo no les creo,
y a donde suelo ir
la encuentro
nuevamente,
molestando con sus
alas.
Y claro
sólo los tontos
compran rejilla con mango,
o un periódico viejo,
y la persiguen

Flies

OK fly,
you fly OK
you draw yourself in the air
tight banks quick turns
graph the walls
with your shadow
and you're laughing at me
and I don't even look at you
settle on my nose
take a trip on my head
settle on my shoulder
and I suppose it amuses you fly
when I try to flatten you
with my slow hand,
sure, settle on my bread
my toast, my books
they're just there for you.
You know,
they tell me you push
some heavy diseases
but I don't believe it
and when I go to piss
there you are again
fixing your wings.
Some fools buy swatters
or chase you
with an old newspaper
just to see you
fall down dead—
that's a job for the idle,
fly killing
          you don't scare
the larger animals
or even dogs.

hasta que la ven caer,
moribunda.
Es oficio de ociosos,
eso de matar moscas
diariamente,
pues Ud., señorita mosca,
no asusta ni a las vacas
ni a los perros.

Pero le advierto:
si algún día yo pudiera,
reuniría a todos los sabios
del mundo,
y les mandaría fabricar
un aparato volador
que acabaría con Ud. y sus
amigos para siempre.
Sólo espero no alimentarla
y no verla en mis entrañas,
el día que si acaso
me matan en el campo
y dejan mi cuerpo bajo el sol.

But I want you to get this:
If someday I could
I'd call in all the experts
in the world
I'd order them to put together
a flying machine your size
to finish you and all your girl friends
for ever—
Because I have this recurrent hope
not to feed you
I don't want to see you
in my entrails
the day they cut me open
in the countryside
and leave my body under the sun.

Poema

Yo no me

río de

la

muerte.

Sucede

simple-

mente,

que no

tengo miedo

de morir

entre

pájaros

y

árboles

Lima, 26 de Set.

Poem

No,

I don't

laugh

at

death.

It's

just

that I'm

not afraid

to die

among

birds

and

trees

Lima, Sept. 26

El nuevo viaje

Hacia
las blancas montañas
que me esperan
debo viajar nuevamente.

Hacia los mismos vientos
y hacia los mismos naranjales
deben mis pies enormes
acaparar las tierras
y tienen mis ojos
que acariciar las parras
de los campos.

Viaje rotundo y solo:
¡qué difícil es dejar
todo abandonado!
¡Qué difícil es vivir
entre ciudades y ciudades,
una calle,
un tranvía,
todo se acumula
para que sobreviva
la eterna estación
del desencanto!

2

No se puede pasear
por las arenas
si existen caracoles
opresores y arañas
submarinas.

The New Journey

Soon I must journey again.
Over there,
towards those white mountains
waiting,
waiting for me.

Towards the same winds
the same orange groves
my feet
must seize the plains
and with my eyes
I want to feel the vines
of the countryside.

A round journey, and alone:
It isn't easy to leave—
everything abandoned!
the difficulty it is to live
in city after city
a street
the streetcar
everything increases the sense
and the endless season
of disenchantment
survives.

2

And you can't go for a walk
along the beaches
if the simple condition
is lethal shells
and submarine spiders.

Y sin embargo,
caminando un poco,
volteando hacia la izquierda,
se llega a las montañas
y a los ríos.
No es que yo quiera
alejarme de la vida,
sino que tengo
que acercarme hacia la muerte.

3

No es que yo quiera
aseguar mis pasos:
a cado rato nos
tienden emboscadas,
a cada rato nos roban
nuestras cartas,
a cada rato nos salen
con engaños.

4

Es mejor: lo recomiendo:
Alejarse por un tiempo
del bullicio
y conocer
las montañas ignoradas.

So, walk on a while
turn to the left
and you reach the mountains
and the rivers.

Look it isn't that I want
to leave life back there—
but I must follow a path
that death is known to stalk.

3

And it isn't that I seek
to protect my step—
at every moment every turn
they set up ambushes for us,
on every occasion they steal
our letters, of course
at every moment they come on
with their tested tricks.

4

But it is better than other ways:
I recommend it—
                    get away for a time
from the bustle
learn what it's all about
in those mountains.

Otto René Castillo

Vamonos patria a caminar

Vámonos patria a caminar, yo te acompaño.

Yo bajaré los abismos que me digas.
Yo beberé tus cálices amargos.
Yo me quedaré ciego para que tengas ojos.
Yo me quedaré sin voz para que tú cantes.
Yo he de morir para que tú no mueras,
para que emerja tu rostro flameando al horizonte
de cada flor que nazca de mis huesos.

Tiene que ser así, indiscutiblemente.

Ya me cansé de llevar tus lágrimas conmigo.
Ahora quiero caminar contigo, relampagueante.
Acompañarte en tu jornada, porque soy un hombre
del pueblo, nacido en octubre para la faz del mundo.
Ay patria,
a los coroneles que orinan tus muros
tenemos que arrancarlos de raíces,
colgarlos en un árbol de rocío agudo,
violento de cóleras del pueblo.
Por ello pido que caminemos juntos. Siempre
con los campesinos agrarios
y los obreros sindicales,
con el que tenga un corazón para quererte.

Vámonos patria a caminar, yo te acompaño.

Otto René Castillo

Let's Start Walking

Let's take a walk Guatemala, I'm coming along.

I'll go down with you, as deep as you say
I'll drink from your bitter cup.
I'll spend my sight so you may have eyes
I'll throw in my voice so you may sing
I'll die to give you life
and your face will be on the bright horizon
in every boll of the flowers born of my bones.

It must be this way, indisputably.

I got tired of carrying your tears around with me.
Now I want to walk with you, strike lightning.
Go to work with you help you do things because I am
one of you, born in October for the face of the world.

O Guatemala,
those colonels who piss on your walls
we must tear out by their roots
and hang them up on a cold tree of dew
shimmering violet with the anger of the people.

I ask to walk with you. Always with
the agrarians and the workers
and with any man who has the presence to love you.

Let's start walking country, I'm coming with you.

Fernando Gordillo Cervantes

Andrés

Andrés,
tu piedra es mi esperanza.
Ha pasado un siglo y ya lo ves,
todo lo mismo.
Pudo más el oro que la sangre.
Toda tu tierra, Andrés,
desde los lagos al Coco,
desde el Cabo hasta el San Juan,
es una sola lágrima donde la Patria llora

Lanza la piedra.
¡Lánzala!
A un siglo de distancia, el enemigo
es el mismo.

Un joven muerto

Un joven muerto, no hiere el corazón de un rifle.
Ni hace sufrir las sombras de la nada.
Pero por sus heridas, un poco de cada
uno se ha escapado, para no volver.

La soledad del héroe, es su mayor
martirio.
Hacedle compañía

Fernando Gordillo Cervantes

Andrés

Andrés,
your rock is my hope.
A century has gone and look
things are the same.
Blood is not the equal of gold.
All your land Andrés
from the lakes to the Coco
from the Cape to San Juan
forms a single tear
the country weeps.

Throw the rock.
Throw it!
One hundred years
        from where you stood, the enemy
is the same.

A Dead Youth

A dead youth. How can he turn the heart of a rifle.
How inflict the shades of nothingness with suffering.
But through his wounds a thing from our lives
escapes, gone over the hill for ever.

The large isolation of the hero is his martyrdom.
Don't walk away from him

El precio de una patria

3.000.000 es el precio de una Patria,
si alguien quiere venderla.

Y hube quien quiso y la vendió.
Más tarde dijeron, que sus hijos
nacieron para cantarla.

Como si la lucha no es el más alto
de los cantos.
Y la muerte el más grande.

Los muertos

Los muertos
sostendrán los brazos del combatiente,
la voz de las multitudes,
la herramienta del campesino.

Los muertos ...

¿Quién sostendrá las manos de los muertos?

The Price of a Country

3,000,000 is the pricemark on a country
if somebody wants to sell it.
and someone wanted to
                          and did.
Later they said
                   his sons
were born just to sing it.

Just as if battle is not the most unmistakable
of songs
or death the most grand.

The Dead

The dead, the dead
will brace the arms of the revolutionary
sustain the voice of the multitudes
guide the plough of the countryman

the dead ...

who's going to hold the hands of the dead?

Ya tú sabes que murió

Ya tú sabes que murió
y sabes donde está la tumba del hermano,
aquel hermano que no tuvo sepultura.
Tú lo sabes
porque tu corazón es tierra que lo cubre
y nuestros días flores nuevas para florecer su tumba.

Marco Antonio Flores

Habana 59

De tanto hablar
quedáronse sin voces las cadenas
se sometió la noche
a la alborada
fuese la muerte
con su doble rabo
huyó la peste
con su sable al hombro
los relojes quedáronse
sin ojos
sin orillas de piel
sin botas negras
quedóse el hambre
sin sus mil testigos
el dueño de la vid sin sus
calzones
y el amo sin su sombra:
                    sin su esclavo

Now You Know He Died

Now you know he died
and you know where your brother's grave is
and you know he had no burial
you know that
because your heart will be
the only earth covering him
and all our days will flower
into new flowers sprung on his grave.

Marco Antonio Flores

Havana 1959

Out of so much talking
the chains lost their voices
night was subjected
to dawn
death took away
its forked tail
plague fled
with his black sabre on his shoulder
clocks became
eyeless
without shores of skin
without black boots
hunger wandered out
leaving behind its thousand witnesses
the owner of the vine lost his
pants
and the master lost his shadow:
                              lost his slave

Otto René el poeta

"Mi amigo es un poeta
muy pálido
muy serio
muy sonriente"

Y te marchaste amigo
Tu aliento era tan fuerte
que penetró la tierra
y la bañó con sangre de tu pecho
Hoy estoy triste
                        hasta el tuétano del alma
Tus ojos se me prenden en la voz
y tu sonrisa
se torna mueca amarga entre mi llanto
Quedó crucificada tu palabra
y resucitará
de los que como tú
echan su vida al fuego de la patria
Tu voz está callada
atronando el espacio de mi sangre
erguida en mi recuerdo
                        más tranquilo
recorriendo las calles
nuevamente
ofreciendo esperanza:
maestro
            compañero
                        camarada

Hoy te lloro y no me da vergüenza
Se avientan los recuerdos en tropel
despedazan el ánimo sereno
y el recuento se impone:
Las palabras no dichas y las dichas los gestos cotidianos
la nostalgia por nuestras cosas idas
los poemas que había que arreglar

Otto René the Poet

"My friend is a poet
very pale
very serious
very smiling"

And you went away friend
Your spirit was so strong
it penetrated the earth
and washed it with the blood of your breast
Now I am sad
              to the marrow of my soul
Your eyes get caught in my voice
and your smile
forms a bitter grimace in my tears
Your word was driven through with nails
and will rise again
out of those like you
who throw their lives onto the fire of our country
Your voice is silent
it fills the space of my blood with thunder
erected in my
              quietest memory
ranging the streets
again
offering hope:
master
       companion
           comrade
Now I weep for you without shame
Memories break loose in a tumult
they shatter the quiet mind
and recounting becomes necessary:
The words not said and those said
the common gestures
the desire for our departed things
the poems there were to be gone over

el vino compartido
las angustias del hambre cotidiana
los sueños mutuos
la siembra siempre fértil de tu voz:
Y estás de pie
                    presente en la nostalgia

Y no se olvidarán las calles
de tus pasos
tu andar era profundo
Se quedará tu voz vibrando
en la canción de nuestro pueblo
en el rancho
en el monte
en la quebrada

Se escuchará al juglar cantando décimas
que digan de tu nombre
de tu sangre
de tu pecho deshecho a culatazos
de tu sonrisa triste
Se quedará tu voz cantando en las espigas
que nazcan de la siembra de tus huesos
Se quedará en la boca
de los niños que nazcan de una aurora proletaria
Se quedará
Se quedará tu voz
para cantar
la muerte de los mártires
el canto de los héroes
el hambre
la injusticia
la victoria!
Se quedará tu voz en el silencio
que acompañe
el requiem de los muertos por la espalda

the partaken wine
the burn of everyday hunger
the mutual dreams
the always fertile seed of your voice:
And you are returned

in nostalgia
And the streets where your steps were
will not be forgotten
your walk was profound
Your voice will vibrate on
in the songs of our people
on the farm
on the hills
in the ravine

The ballad singer will be heard singing
of your name
of your blood
of your breast smashed by gun butts
of your sad smile
Your voice will be a song in the ears of wheat
which spring from your broadcast bones
It will be present in the mouths
of children born in a proletarian dawn
It will be there
Your voice will be there
to sing the death
of the martyrs
the song of the heroes
of hunger
injustice
victory!
Your voice will be there in the silence
which travels
through the requiem for those shot in the back

Poeta
combatiente
amigo mío
al pie de tu sonrisa destrozada
elevo mi dolor
y mi protesta
maldigo a los que hirieron tu esperanza
y no te digo adiós
tu nombre está velando
Tu perfil campesino deambulará
en la cara de tus hijos
a la orilla del Elba
en un mundo feliz y liberado
El eco de tu voz comprometida
se hará el catecismo de los míos
y de todos los hijos de tu pueblo
Poeta
amigo mío
heroica semilla proletaria:
desde el pico más alto de la sierra
el tum está doblando
por tu muerte

Requiem por Luis Augusto

I

Les fue dada la acción
de la ceniza
y contaminaron el humus
A pesar de todo
los hombres
hicieron surcos

Poet
fighter
my friend
at the foot of your ruined smile
I raise my pain
and my protest
upon those who wounded your hope I place a curse
and I do not say goodbye to you
your name watches
Your peasant profile will pass
into the faces of your children
on the bank of the Elba
in a happy and liberated world
The echo of your engaged voice
will become the catechism of my children
and of all the children of your people
Poet
my dear friend
heroic proletary seed:
from the highest peak of the sierra
the tum is tolling
for your death

Requiem for Luis Augusto

I

They had the effect
of ash
and they contaminated the humus
Despite everything that had been done
men
made furrows

y metieron la mano en el rescoldo
Pero el crimen
era mucho más hondo
A pesar de él
"esta humanidad ha dicho
¡basta!
y ha echado a andar"
Mientras tanto
seguimos restregándonos
en miedo en justificaciones
Las conchas se siguen redondeando
alrededor del hambre
de los otros
y no somos capaces
de gritar o de poner el pecho
Nuestro es el tiempo de la rapiña de pocos
"Puedo morir mañana
pero otros me sustituirán"
Los ídolos sollozaron
su partida

2

Un menor de cinco años
muere de hambre:
violencia al pueblo
Equitativa y santa
la oferta y la demanda
Un gordo se revienta
con su gula pegada a la chequera
El altiplano gotea sus coyotes
sus altísimos edificios
sus pieles de mink
sus cadillacs
Las viejas gotean

thrust their hands into the embers
But the wrong
was deeper, much deeper
Despite it
"mankind has said
Enough!
and has begun to move"
In the meantime
we go on snagging ourselves
on fear, on justifications
Oyster shells
go on
swelling their form
around the hunger
of others
still we are incapable
of shouting or letting our chests out
Ours is the time of the few who prey
"I may die tomorrow
but others will take my place"
The idols saw him leave
and wept

2

A child not yet 5 years old
dies of hunger:
violence to the people
Equitable and sacred
supply and demand
A fat man bursts
engorged inside his cheque book
The plateau secretes its coyotes
its elevated buildings
its mink coats
its cadillacs
The old ladies drip

su piedad senilmente
en los bailes de caridad:
Es antiquísimo el dolor

                 no perpetuo

Nuestro es el tiempo
de las depredaciones
Pero "esta humanidad ha dicho
¡basta!
y ha echado a andar"

     3

Usurpamos esta tranquilidad
de comprar alimentos
Enfrente hay otra cara
llena de mal de pobre
Tengo miedo pero no terror
El terror vence al hombre
El hombre vence al miedo
Voy a pararme en medio
de los vientos
a vendimiar mi piel
Después me arrastraré
Colocaré mi nombre en las raíces
y las enterraré muy hondo

                entre las aguas

Desde el pico
más alto
se tenderá la red
que sostendrá nuestros sueños

     4

"Puedo morir mañana
pero otros me sustituirán"
Una muchacha llora

their pity tottering
at their charity balls:
The pain is of great antiquity

                     but not eternal

Ours is the time
of plunder
Yes "mankind has said
Enough!
and has begun to move"

     3

We are usurpers of the easiness
of buying food
Across from us is another face
full of hunger's disease
I am afraid but not terrified
Terror conquers man
Man subjugates fear
I am going to stand
in the eye of the wind
to kill my flesh
Then I intend
over the ground
to drag myself
To place my name in the roots
to bury those roots very deep

                    in the watertable

From the highest peak
the net will stretch there
that holds our dreams

     4

"I may die tomorrow
but others will take my place"
A girl weeps

el abandono
Eran sus ojos
los de un ajusticiado
El sol vuelve a salir
No es un árbol
el que dará la sombra
Es el bosque
No habrá que confundirse ni llorar
La rosa germina
avanza amparada en la maleza
La juventud se marcha
para arriba
        —o para abajo—
Del monte bajan
los torrentes
de geranios
que saludan
empuñando la diestra

La gente sigue autómata
a pesar del cuchillo
de la muerte
Los petardos resuenan
más sonoros
en medio de la noche
Las esquinas se esconden
en la casa del sol
La multitud aúlla de temor
Los amigos regalan
sus arterias
al lobo
aparecen torcidos
en páginas pedestres
quebrados por las balas
Sólo hay una respuesta:
la violencia

in her bereavement, abandoned
His eyes were eyes
as an executed man has eyes
Again the sun is out
It is not a tree
which casts the shade
It is the wood
You must not be confused or cry
The rose germinates
and climbs
protected in the underbush
Young men take themselves off
by the uplands
                    or by the lowlands
And down from the hills
come torrents
of geraniums
which salute you
clenching their right hands

People go on being automatons
even when the knife
of death
rips
more audible
in the mid night
The street's corners hide
in the house of the sun
The multitude howls in terror
Friends give
their arteries
to the wolf for nothing
and appear then
on pedestrian pages
busted by bullets
There is one response only:
Violence

5

"Puedo morir mañana
pero otros me sustituirán"
Eran sus ojos
los de un ajusticiado
Lloró el asfalto
en su costado
Mientras tanto
                        nosotros
decimos disfrutar
el sueldo mendrugado
Nos contentamos con bajar
la cabeza
ante su muerte
y sollozar hipócritas
No es nuestro el tiempo
de la espera
Su garganta quemada
propagó la mañana que entreabre los dedos
El silencio ahorca los sueños
Todo es ausencia

Despedida al que fui

Los adioses se pierden en los pájaros que parten
y en los días que se van al pasado
de repente se olvidan
se mueren
Así el adios que aleje tu presencia
Partiré la más pequeña arena de esta playa
y te daré una parte
Mi parte será mi compañera
el templo de mi lucha
mi coraza

5

"I may die tomorrow
but others will take my place"
His eyes were the eyes
of an executed man
The asphalt wept fire
in his side
In the meantime
                  all of us
say we enjoy
our crust-of-bread paycheck
We are contented and lower
our heads
to his death
content to sob hypocritically
It is not ours, this waiting time
His burnt throat
propagated the morning which half unbends our fingers
Silence slaughters dreams
All is absence

Goodbye to the Man I Was

Goodbyes lose themselves with the departing birds
and in the days which float into the past
they are forgotten suddenly
they die in themselves
And so the goodbye upon which your presence embarks
I shall divide the smallest arena on this beach
and I shall give you a part of it
My part will be my woman
the marked space of my struggle
my cuirass

Las voces del aire conocen el turbión
de mi morada más honda

Una sonaja de chayes en mis cuencas
escupen sus destellos
alumbran un camino sin veredas
sin árboles
sin abrazos que dar

Michele Najlis

A Fernando

Si me ves en las calles llena de sonrisas
si amo los ojos de un niño
recuerda que descubrimos paso a paso
el mundo que me enseñaste
recuerda que mi mano permanece en tu mano
y que mi cuerpo se detiene en tu presencia:
piensa que el amor termina donde empieza el vacío
y juntos matamos el vacío

The voices of the wind know the turbulence
of my deepest dwelling

Obsidian maracas in the sockets of my eyes
spit out their sparks
illuminate a road without sidewalks
without trees
without embraces to give

Michele Najlis

To Fernando

If you see me in the street
       full of smiles
If I love the eyes of a child
       remember
we rediscover
       step by step
the world you showed me
and remember my hand
       is in your hand still
and remember my body
       is the hammock of your presence

think of this—love ends
where the void begins
and we pierce the void together.

Pablo Hernando Guerrero

No te escondas compañero

Hoy es dura
esa amante a quien tanto le hicimos el amor
esa amante américa,
de un solo beso la llegaste a recorrer
y te hundiste en sus montañas
y en las manos un fusil que disparaba,
                    montaste sus barcas
con un caballo de nombre Fidel
aquel 26 desembarcaste en un prostíbulo
                    y del granma y del lagarto
salió el hombre reventando la sierra.
No sabías de estrategia
                    no mientas che
conocías al hombre y su enemigo
y predecíamos ese primero del año
                    cuando desde
un caballo y mil barbas entraste a construir
un hombre virgen.

Ser Continental
compartes con Camilo tierras
ustedes dos gigantes
de nuevo se esconden en las vértebras del árbol
y tal vez un día igual al de ayer (pero sin Cristóbal)
cuando el grande río nos cubra de ira
                    surgirán
y con nuestras manos alimentaremos la nueva canción.

Vos con Camilo,
más corta su presencia para un rápido futuro
hacen su guerrilla cada vez más invisible
y mientras tanto
                    aquí ...

Pablo Hernando Guerrero

Don't Hide

She's hard today
that lover we lay with so much
that American lover
you spread with one kiss all over her
and plunged yourself between her mountains
and in your hands a gun discharging

                           got into her ships

with a horse named Fidel
that 26 July you disembarked
on to a whorehouse

            and out of Granma
            and from Lagarto

man came crushing the sierra.
It wasn't about strategy

                  don't put me on, Che,

you knew about man—and his enemy
and we foresaw that New Year

            when from

a horse and a thousand beards you arrived
to make man virgin again.

Man of the hemisphere
you share the ground with Camilo
and are giant with him
hiding again now in the tree's vertebrae
and maybe one day like yesterday

                  (but without Cristobal this time)

when the wide river covers us with wrath

            you will both arrive

and with our hands we shall feed the new song.

You and Camilo,
the quickness of your presence for a fast future

hay un disco hereje
que se escucha como víspera.

Endnotes to *Palabra de Guerrillero*

From *Our Word, Guerrilla Poems from Latin America/Palabra de guerrillero: Poesia guerrillera de Latinoamerica* (Cape Goliard: London, 1968).

86. This anonymous poem is taken from a mimeographed student broadsheet, *Rebelion* (Trujillo, February 1966). Luis de la Puente was the leader of the Peruvian Movimiento de Izquierda Revolucionaria (MIR); he was betrayed by a guide and killed in 1965.

108. Andrés Castro, a Nicaraguan hero, fought against the U.S. invaders under the command of William Walker in the Hacienda de San Jacinto. Lacking munitions, Andrés seized a rock and with it knocked down the first Yankee who tried to cross the barricade that protected the hacienda.

110. About the events (and the attitudes which made these events possible) which led to the conclusion of the 1916 Bryan-Chamorro treaty between Nicaragua and the U.S.A.

115. "Otto René the Poet": Otto René Castillo

120. "coyotes": a term of Nahuatl origin which is used derogatively in Mexico and Central America to denote Latinos and whites.

128. "sonaja de chayes": Maya in origin, "chay" is the word for obsidian—and for knives, mirrors, and other artifacts made from that material.

130: "Camilo": Camilo Torres, a co-revolutionary.

your guerrilla war progressively invisible
and here meanwhile
there is an unorthodox gramophone
heard like the eve of a new day.

Che Ernesto Guevara was born and educated in Argentina; while a
medical student, he motor-biked throughout South America, wit-
nessing the appalling poverty and social blight brought about by
governments. A poet, intellectual, and scientist, Guevara met Fidel
Castro in Mexico City, took up the cause of armed struggle, crossed
the water with the revolutionary army on the Granma to Cuba, and
fought alongside el Comandante in the Sierra Madres. A major force
in the 1959 Cuban Revolution, he served as Minister of Industry for
five years before his restless spirit directed him again to the jungle.
In October, 1967, at the age of 39, he and his small band of guerril-
las were ambushed in Bolivia. Executed a few days later, Guevara
was mourned around the world as a great revolutionary hero. His
mutilated remains were recently dug up in Bolivia and flown to
Havana, where they were reburied with the honor he deserved. This
poem was written on the eve of his embarkation with Fidel to Cuba.

Luis Nieto, born in Peru in 1910, contributed many poems to the
revolutionary struggle in his country.

Javier Heraud became a student at the Universidad Católica in 1958
and won a national poetry prize with his second book of poems *El
viaje*. After studying cinema in Cuba, he returned to Peru and joined
the Ejército de Liberación Nacional as a guerrilla. He was shot to
death in 1963, in the middle of the river Madre de Dios.

Otto René Castillo, a Guatemalan student organizer from 1954, was
exiled for the first time at the age of 17. During the next ten years

he was tortured and imprisoned several times—but managed to study both at the University of Guatemala and at the University of Leipzig. In 1955 he shared the premio Centroamericana de Poesía with the Salvadorian poet Roque Dalton. Castillo came back to Guatemala for the last time in 1966 and joined the ranks of F.A.R. (Fuerzas Armadas Revolucionarias). In March 1967, after eating nothing but roots for 15 days, his guerrilla group was ambushed and captured. After four days of torture Castillo was put to death and burnt.

Fernando Gordillo Cervantes was a Nicaraguan guerrilla soldier, an essayist, and a writer of poems and short stories. Known for his bravery and his leadership of his fellow students, he died on July 24, 1967.

Marco Antonio Flores, a Guatemalan poet, wrote several books of poetry and directed theater in Havana and Guatemala City.

Michele Najlis, a prominent Nicaraguan leader, addressed this poem to Fernando Gordillo Cervantes.

Pablo Hernando Guerrero participated in the Cuban Revolution and became a member of the Cuban Government.

MODERN CHRONICLES

CESAR VALLEJO

LOS HERALDOS NEGROS

Los heraldos negros

Hay golpes en la vida, tan fuertes ... Yo no sé!
Golpes como del odio de Dios; como si ante ellos,
la resaca de todo lo sufrido
se empozara en el alma ... Yo no sé!

Son pocos; pero son ... Abren zanjas oscuras
en el rostro más fiero y en el lomo más fuerte.
Serán talvez los potros de bárbaros atilas;
o los heraldos negros que nos manda la Muerte.

Son las caídas hondas de los Cristos del alma,
de alguna fe adorable que el Destino blasfema.
Esos golpes sangrientos son las crepitaciones
de algún pan que en la puerta del horno se nos quema.

Y el hombre ... Pobre ... pobre! Vuelve los ojos, como
cuando por sobre el hombro nos llama una palmada;
vuelve los ojos locos, y todo lo vivido
se empoza, como charco de culpa, en la mirada.

Hay golpes en la vida, tan fuertes ... Yo no sé!

Ágape

Hoy no ha venido nadie a preguntar;
ni me han pedido en esta tarde nada.

No he visto ni una flor de cementerio
en tan alegre procesión de luces.
Perdóname, Señor: qué poco he muerto!

THE BLACK HERALDS

The black heralds

There are knocks in life, so hard ... I don't know!
Knocks like God's hate; as if under them
the backwash of everything suffered
had stagnated in your soul ... I don't know!

They are few; but they are ... They open dark weals
in the keenest face, in the hardest back.
They could be the colts of wild Attilas;
or the black heralds death sends us.

They are the deep chutes of your soul Christs,
of some pretty faith Destiny blasphemes.
Those bloodied knocks are the crackling
of a loaf that burns up at the oven door.

And man ... Poor man! He turns his eyes as
when a clap on the shoulder summons us;
he turns his mad eyes, and everything lived
stagnates like a guilt pond in his look.

There are knocks in life, so hard ... I don't know!

Agape

Today no-one has come to inquire;
they haven't this evening asked anything of me.

I haven't seen a single cemetery flower
in such a gay procession of lights.
Forgive me, Lord; how little I have died.

En esta tarde todos, todos pasan
sin preguntarme ni pedirme nada.

Y no sé qué se olvidan y se queda
mal en mis manos, como cosa ajena.

He salido a la puerta,
y me da ganas de gritar a todos:
Si echan de menos algo, aquí se queda!

Porque en todas las tardes de esta vida,
yo no sé con qué puertas dan a un rostro,
y algo ajeno se toma el alma mía.

Hoy no ha venido nadie;
y hoy he muerto qué poco en esta tarde!

Los dados eternos

Para Manuel González Prada esta emoción bravía y
selecta, una de las que, con más entusiasmo, me ha
aplaudido el gran maestro

Dios mío, estoy llorando el ser que vivo;
me pesa haber tomádote tu pan;
pero este pobre barro pensativo
no es costra fermentada en tu costado:
tú no tienes Marías que se van!

Dios mío, si tú hubieras sido hombre,
hoy supieras ser Dios;
pero tú, que estuviste siempre bien,
no sientes nada de tu creación.
Y el hombre sí te sufre: el Dios es él!

Hoy que en mis ojos brujos hay candelas,

On this evening everyone, everyone goes by
not inquiring or asking anything of me.

And I don't know what they forget and is left
wrong in my hands, like someone else's thing.

I've gone out to the door
and would shout to them all:
If you miss anything, it's here!

Because on all the evenings of this life,
I don't know what doors get slammed in my face,
and something alien seizes my soul.

Today no-one has come by:
and today I have died how little on this evening.

The eternal dice

*For Manuel González Prada, this unbridled select
emotion, one of those the great master has applauded
in me with most enthusiasm*

My god, I mourn the being I live;
I regret I took your bread;
but this poor thinking clay
is not a scab fermented in your side:
you don't have Marys who go away!

My God, had you been a man,
you'd know today how to be God;
but you who were always free
feel nothing of what you made.
And man does suffer you: the God is he!

Today there's a glow in my witch eye

como en un condenado,
Dios mío, prenderás todas tus velas,
y jugaremos con el viejo dado …
Talvez ¡oh jugador! al dar la suerte
del universo todo,
surgirán las ojeras de la Muerte,
como dos ases fúnebres de lodo.

Dios mío, y esta noche sorda, oscura,
ya no podrás jugar, porque la Tierra
es un dado roído y ya redondo
a fuerza de rodar a la aventura,
que no puede parar sino en un hueco,
en el hueco de inmensa sepultura.

A mi hermano Miguel
in memoriam

Hermano, hoy estoy en el poyo de la casa,
donde nos haces una falta sin fondo!
Me acuerdo que jugábamos esta hora, y que mamá
nos acariciaba : "Pero, hijos … "

Ahora yo me escondo,
como antes, todas estas oraciones
vespertinas, y espero que tú no des conmingo.
Por la sala, el zaguán, los corredores.
Después, te ocultas tú, y yo no doy contigo.
Me acuerdo que nos hacíamos llorar,
hermano, en aquel juego.

Miguel, tú te escondiste
una noche de agosto, al alborear;
pero, en vez de ocultarte riendo, estabas triste.
Y tu gemelo corazón de esas tardes

as in a man damned to death
so you, my God, will light your candles all
and we'll play with the old die ...
Could be, oh gambler, when the mortal
lot of the whole universe falls,
the full eyes of Death shall
show like two funereal aces of mud.

My god, and this dull night of gloom
how will you play, for the Earth
is a worn die, already round
from rolling at random,
and cannot stop but in a hollow,
in the hollow of an immense tomb.

To my brother Miguel
in memoriam

Brother, today I'm on the bench by the door,
and here we miss you terribly.
I remember we used to play at this hour, Mummy
would caress us : "But, children ... "

Now I go and hide,
as before, all these even-
songs, and hope you don't discover me.
Through the drawing room, the hall, the corridors.
Then you hide, and I can't find you.
I remember we made each other cry,
brother, with that game.

Miguel, you hid
one August night, at first light;
but instead of vanishing in fun, you were sad.
And your twin heart of those extinct

extintas se ha aburrido de no encontrarte. Y ya
cae sombra en el alma.

Oye, hermano, no tardes
en salir. Bueno? Puede inquietarse mamá.

Espergesia

Yo nací un día
que Dios estuvo enfermo.

Todos saben que vivo,
que soy malo; y no saben
del diciembre de ese enero.
Pues yo nací un día
que Dios estuvo enfermo.

Hay un vacío
en mi aire metafísico
que nadie ha de palpar:
el claustro de un silencio
que habló a flor de fuego.
Yo nací un día
que Dios estuvo enfermo.

Hermano, escucha, escucha ...
Bueno. Y que no me vaya
sin llevar diciembres,
sin dejar eneros.
Pues yo nací un día
que Dios estuvo enfermo.

Todos saben que vivo,
que mastico ... Y no saben
por qué en mi verso chirrían,

evenings got tired of not finding you. And now
shadow falls into the soul.

Hey, brother, don't be too long
coming out. All right? Mummy might get worried.

Verdict

I was born one day
when God was ill.

Everyone knows I live,
that I'm bad; and they don't know
about the December of that January.
For I was born one day
when God was ill.

There's a hole
in my metaphysical air
no-one shall feel:
the cloister of a silence
that spoke flush with fire.
I was born one day
when God was ill.

Listen, brother, listen ...
All right. And don't let me go
not bringing Decembers,
not leaving Januaries.
For I was born one day
when God was ill.

Everyone knows I live,
that I chew ... And they don't know
why in my verse creak

oscuro sinsabor de féretro,
luyidos vientos
desenroscados de la Esfinge
preguntona del Desierto.

Todos saben ... Y no saben
que la Luz es tísica,
y la Sombra gorda ...
Y no saben que el Misterio sintetiza ...
que él es la joroba
musical y triste que a distancia denuncia
el paso meridiano de las lindes a las Lindes.

Yo nací un día
que Dios estuvo enfermo,
grave.

TRILCE

I

Quién hace tánta bulla, y ni deja
testar las islas que van quedando.

Un poco más de consideración
en cuanto será tarde, temprano,
y se aquilatará, mejor
el guano, la simple calabrina tesórea
que brinda sin querer,
en el insular corazón,
salobre alcatraz, a cada hialóidea
　　　grupada.

Un poco más de consideración

dark whiffs of the hearse
chafed winds
uncoiling from the Sphinx
pry of the Desert.

Everyone knows ... And they don't know
that the Light is consumptive,
and the Shade fat ...
And they don't know the Mystery synthesizes ...
or who is the sad musical
hump that denounces from far
the meridian step from bourne to Bourne.

I was born one day
when God was seriously
ill.

TRILCE

I

Who is it so shrill, and who keeps
the remaining islands from their last will.

A little more consideration
whether sooner or later,
and the guano will be more finely
assayed, the simple treasurey brew
which the salty pelican can't help propining,
on the island's heart,
with each hyaloid
                    squall.

A little more consideration,

y el mantillo líquido, seis de la tarde
DE LOS MAS SOBERBIOS BEMOLES.

Y la península párase
por la espalda, abozaleada, impertérrita
en la línea mortal del equilibrio.

II

Tiempo Tiempo

Mediodía estancado entre relentes.
Bomba aburrida del cuartel achica
tiempo tiempo tiempo tiempo.

Era Era.

Gallos cancionan escarbando en vano.
Boca del claro día que conjuga
era era era era.

Mañana Mañana.

El reposo caliente aun de ser.
Piensa el presente guárdame para
mañana mañana mañana mañana.

Nombre Nombre.

¿Qué se llama cuanto heriza nos?
Se llama Lomismo que padece
nombre nombre nombrE

and liquid dung, six in the evening
　　OF THE MOST SUPERB B-FLATS.

And the peninsula gets ready
on its back, muzzled, serene
on the dead line of balance.

　　II

　　Time Time

Midday fothered between dews.
Bored lightbulb in the barracks shrinks
time time time time

　　Was Was

Cocks chant scratching in vain.
Mouth of the clear day that conjugates
was was was was

　　Morrow Morrow

The warm repose of being yet.
The present thinks keep me for to
morrow morrow morrow morrow

　　Name Name

What's all that pricks us called?
It's called Samething as suffers
name name namE

III

Las personas mayores
¿a qué hora volverán?
Da las seis el ciego Santiago,
y ya está muy oscuro.

Madre dijo que no demoraría.

Aguedita, Nativa, Miguel,
cuidado con ir por ahí, por donde
acaban de pasar gangueando sus memorias
dobladoras penas,
hacia el silencioso corral, y por donde
las gallinas que se están acostando todavía,
se han espantado tanto.
Mejor estemos aquí no más.
Madre dijo que no demoraría.

Ya no tengamos pena. Vamos viendo
los barcos ¡el mío es más bonito de todos!
con los cuales jugamos todo el santo día,
sin pelearnos, como debe de ser:
han quedado en el pozo de agua, listos,
fletados de dulces para mañana.

Aguardemos así, obedientes y sin más
remedio, la vuelta, el desagravio
de los mayores siempre delanteros
dejándonos en casa a los pequeños,
como si también nosotros
                    no pudiésemos partir.

Aguedita, Nativa, Miguel?
Llamo, busco al tanteo en la oscuridad.
No me vayan a haber dejado solo,
y el único recluso sea yo.

III

Our parents
what time will they be back?
Blind Santiago is ringing six,
and it's already very dark.

Mother said she wouldn't be long.

Aguedita, Nativa, Miguel,
mind how you go there, where
the doubling ghosts
have passed through twanging their memories
towards the silent yard, and where
the hens are still settling down,
they were so scared.
Better just stay here,
Mother said she wouldn't be long.

Let's not fret anymore. We'll take a look
at the boats, mine's the prettiest of all,
the ones we played with the whole day through,
no quarreling, the way it ought to be:
they're still on the pond, ready,
with their cargo of sweets for tomorrow.

Let's wait like this, obedient and with
no other choice, for
the return, the making amends
of our parents always up front
always leaving us at home,
as if we could not
                    go away too.

Aguedita, Nativa, Miguel?
I call, I feel my way in the dark.
They can't have left me alone,
the only prisoner here can't be me.

V

Grupo dicotiledón. Oberturan
desde él petreles, propensiones de trinidad
finales que comienzan, ohs de ayes
creyérase avaloriados de heterogeneidad.
¡Grupo de los dos cotiledones!

A ver. Aquello sea sin ser más.
A ver. No trascienda hacia afuera,
y piense en són de no ser escuchado,
y crome y no sea visto.
Y no glise en el gran colapso.

La creada voz rebélase y no quiere
ser malla, ni amor.
Los novios sean novios en eternidad.
Pues no deis 1, que resonará al infinito.
Y no deis 0, que callará tanto,
hasta despertar y poner de pie al 1.

Ah grupo bicardiaco.

VI

El traje que vestí mañana
no lo ha lavado mi lavandera:
lo lavaba en sus venas otilinas,
en el chorro de su corazón, y hoy no he
de preguntarme si yo dejaba
el traje turbio de injusticia.

Ahora que no hay quien vaya a las aguas,
en mis falsillas encañona
el lienzo para emplumar, y todas las cosas
del velador de tanto qué será de mí,

V

Dicotyledon clutch. From here
petrels overture, a swell towards trinity
ends that begin, ohs from ahs
like they were enhanced with heterogeneity.
Clutch of the two cotyledons!

OK. Let that thing be without being more.
OK. Don't let it transcend outwards,
and let it think the way no-one listens to,
and let it chromate and not be seen.
And don't let it slide into the great collapse.

The created voice rebels and wants not
to be chain-mail, or amour.
May these lovers be switched into eternity.
So don't give I it will resound ad infinitum.
And don't give O because O will be so silent
as to awaken I and stand it up.

Ah bicardiac clutch.

VI

The suit I wore tomorrow
my washerwoman has not washed:
once she washed it in her otiline veins,
in the fountain of her heart, and today
I'd better not wonder   was I leaving
my suit muddy with injustice.

Now that there's no one going to the water,
the canvas for pluming stiffens in
my sampler, and all the things
on the night-table from so much what'll become of me,

todas no están mías
a mi lado.

Quedaron de su propiedad,
fratesadas, selladas con su trigueña bondad.

Y si supiera si ha de volver;
y si supiera qué mañana entrará
a entregarme las ropas lavadas, mi aquella
lavandera del alma. Qué mañana entrará
satisfecha, capulí de obrería, dichosa
de probar que sí sabe, que sí puede
         ¡COMO NO VA PODER!
azular y planchar todos los caos.

VII

Rumbé sin novedad por la veteada calle
que yo me sé. Todo sin novedad,
de veras. Y fondeé hacia cosas así,
y fui pasado.

Doblé la calle por la que raras
veces se pasa con bien, salida
heroica por la herida de aquella
esquina viva, nada a medias.

Son los grandores,
el grito aquel, la claridad de careo,
la barreta sumersa en su función de
                              ¡ya!

Cuando la calle está ojerosa de puertas,
y pregona desde descalzos atriles
trasmañanar las salvas en los dobles.

are all not mine there
at my side.

They remained her property,
smoothed down, brothersealed with her wheat goodness.

And if only I knew whether she'll come back;
and if only I knew what morrow she'll come in
and hand me my washed clothes, that soul
washerwoman of mine. What morrow she'll come in
satisfied, blooming with handiwork, happy
at proving she *does* know, that she is able
       LIKE HOW COULDN'T SHE BE!
to blue and iron out all chaos.

VII

I was off as usual along the veined street
which I know too well. Nothing happening,
really. And I sapped towards things like that,
and was past.

I turned along the street
one rarely walks with ease, a heroic
exit through the wound
of that living corner, nothing halfway.

These are the bags,
the streetcry, the fame of the probe,
the crow that fits in its total
                    right!

When the street is full-eyed with doors,
and proclaims from discalced lecterns
the morning salvo's regress to the knell.

Ahora hormigas minuteras
se adentran dulzoradas, dormitadas, apenas
dispuestas, y se baldan,
quemadas pólveras, altos de a   1921.

VIII

Mañana esotro día, alguna
vez hallaría para el hifalto poder,
entrada eternal.

Mañana algún día,
sería la tienda chapada
con un par de pericardios, pareja
de carnívoros en celo.

Bien puede afincar todo eso.
Pero un mañana sin mañana,
entre los aros de que enviudemos,
margen de espejo habrá
donde traspasaré mi propio frente
hasta perder el eco
y quedar con el frente hacia la espalda.

IX

Vusco volvvver de golpe el golpe.
Sus dos hojas anchas, su válvula
que se abre en suculenta recepción
de multiplicando a multiplicador,
su condición excelente para el placer,
todo avía verdad.

Busco volver de golpe el golpe.
A su halago, enveto bolivarianas fragosidades

Now the minute-hand ants
go deeper sweetened, dozing, ill
prepared, and waste themselves,
burned-out powder, highs in   1921.

VIII

Tomorrow th'other day, some
where for lackheir power would find,
entry unlimited.

Tomorrow some day,
would be the shop boarded up
with two heart sacs, a couple
of meat eaters in heat.

May well get established all that.
But one tomorrow without a morrow,
between the hoops we may bereave,
there'll be a mirror edge
I'll put my own brow through
until I lose the echo
and remain with my brow to my back.

IX

Vvaliant I strivve to back the blow.
Her broad double leaves, her valve
which opens in succulent admission
from multiplicand to multiplier,
her condition excellent with pleasure,
the whole guaranteed truth.

Valiant I strivve to back the blow.
In her coming I open bolivarian veins

a treintidós cables y sus múltiples,
se arrequintan pelo por pelo
soberanos belfos, los dos tomos de la Obra,
y no vivo entonces ausencia,
                 ni al tacto.

Fallo bolver de golpe el golpe.
No ensillaremos jamás el toroso. Vaveo
de egoísmo y de aquel ludir mortal
de sábana,
desque la mujer esta
                 ¡cuanto pesa de general!

Y hembra es el alma de la ausente.
Y hembra es el alma mía.

XIII

Pienso en tu sexo.
Simplificado el corazón, pienso en tu sexo,
ante el hijar maduro del día.
Palpo el botón de dicha, está en sazón.
Y muere un sentimiento antiguo
degenerado en seso.

Pienso en tu sexo, surco más prolífico
y armonioso que el vientre de la Sombra,
aunque la Muerte concibe y pare
de Dios mismo.
Oh Conciencia,
pienso, sí, en el bruto libre
que goza donde quiere, donde puede.

Oh, escándalo de miel de los crepúsculos.
Oh estruendo mudo.

¡Odumodneurtse!

for 32 furlongs and their five multiples,
hair by hair the horse lipped lords are ploughed
the two books of the Work,
and then I am not an absentee,
          not even to the touch.

I fail to back the blow.
Saddle the bullhip we never shall. I foam
from egoism and the desolate loss
on the sheet,
for this woman
          how she weighs!

And female is the soul of the absent one.
And female is my soul.

        XIII

I think of your sex.
With my heart simplified, I think of your sex,
before the mature childing of the day.
I touch the bud of happiness, it's in season.
And an old brainsix
feeling dies.

I think of your sex, a furrow more prolific
and harmonious than the belly of the Shade,
though Death conceives and bears
by God himself.
Oh Conscience,
I think (it's true) of the free brute
who enjoys what he wants and where he can.

Oh, scandal of twilight honey.
Oh inaudible roar.

Raorelbiduani!

XIV

Cual mi explicación.
Esto me lacera de tempranía.
Esa manera de caminar por los trapecios.
Esos corajosos brutos como postizos.
Esa goma que pega el azogue al adentro.
Esas posaderas sentadas para arriba.

Ese no puede ser, sido.

Absurdo.

Demencia.

Pero he venido de Trujillo a Lima.
Pero gano un sueldo de cinco soles.

XV

En el rincón aquel, donde dormimos juntos
tantas noches, ahora me he sentado
a caminar. La cuja de los novios difuntos
fue sacada, o talvez qué habrá pasado.

Has venido temprano a otros asuntos
y ya no estás. Es el rincón
donde a tu lado, leí una noche,
entre tus tiernos puntos,
un cuento de Daudet. Es el rincón
amado. No lo equivoques.

Me he puesto a recordar los días
de verano idos, tu entrar y salir,
poca y harta y pálida por los cuartos.

XIV

Like my explanation.
This lacerates me with earliness.
That way of walking along trapezes.
Those angry brutes like switches of hair.
That gum which sticks the quicksilver to the inside.
Those butts seated upwards.

That cannot be, been.

Absurd.

Dementia.

But I've come from Trujillo to Lima.
But I'm getting a wage of five soles.

XV

In that corner, where we slept together
so many nights, now I have sat down
to walk. The bed of the dead lovers
was taken out, or maybe what can have happened.

You've come early on other business
and now you've gone. It's the corner
where at your side I read one night,
between your tender points,
a story by Daudet. It's the loved
corner. Don't mistake it.

I have got down to recalling the days
of summer gone, your coming in and your going out
few and sated and pale through the rooms.

En esta noche pluviosa,
y lejos de ambos dos, salto de pronto ...
Son dos puertas abriéndose cerrándose,
dos puertas que al viento van y vienen
sombra   a   sombra

XVIII

Oh las cuatro paredes de la celda.
Ah las cuatro paredes albicantes
que sin remedio dan al mismo número.

Criadero de nervios, mala brecha,
por sus cuatro rincones cómo arranca
las diarias aherrojadas extremidades.

Amorosa llavera de innumerables llaves,
si estuvieras aquí, si vieras hasta
qué hora son cuatro estas paredes.
Contra ellas seríamos contigo, los dos,
más dos que nunca. Y ni lloraras,
di, libertadora!

Ah las paredes de la celda.
De ellas me duelen entretanto más
las dos largas que tienen esta noche
algo de madres que ya muertas
llevan por bromurados declives,
a un niño de la mano cada una.

Y sólo yo me voy quedando,
con la diestra, que hace por ambas manos,
en alto, en busca de terciario brazo
que ha de pupilar, entre mi dónde y mi cuándo,
esta mayoría inválida de hombre.

In this humid night,
now far from both of us, I start up ...
It's two doors opening closing,
two doors that come and go in the wind
shadow   to   shadow.

XVIII

The four walls of the cell.
Ah, white totality
irremediably the same number.

Cauldron of nerves, hot spot,
how its four corners tear
out daily rusted limbs.

Loving woman with numberless keys,
if you were here, if you could see how
the walls are forever four.
Against them we'd be with you, the two of us,
more together than ever. And you'd not weep,
speak, Liberté.

The walls of the cell.
Meanwhile the longest two hurt me most
having something tonight
of mothers who already dead
lead down bromide slopes
each one a child by the hand.

And here I am alone,
my right hand, which does for both,
searching all above me for a third arm
to tutor, between my where and my when,
this invalid manhood.

XXII

Es posible me persigan hasta cuatro
magistrados vuelto. Es posible me juzguen
                                        pedro.
¡Cuatro humanidades justas juntas!
Don Juan Jacobo está en hacerio,
y las burlas le tiran de su soledad,
como a un tonto. Bien hecho.

Farol rotoso, el día induce a darle algo,
y pende
a modo de asterisco que se mendiga
a sí propio quizás que enmendaturas.

Ahora que chirapa tan bonito
en esta paz de una sola línea,
aquí me tienes,
aquí me tienes, de quien yo penda,
para que sacies mis esquinas.

Y si, éstas colmadas,
te derramases de mayor bondad,
sacaré de donde no haya,
forjaré de locura otros posíllos,
insaciables ganas
de nivel y amor.

Si pues siempre salimos al encuentro
de cuanto entra por otro lado,
ahora, chirapado eterno y todo,
heme, de quien yo penda,
estoy de filo todavía. Heme!

XXII

It's possible as many as four magistrates
follow me after my release. It's possible they name me
                                                        pietro.

Four fat ones joined exactly!
M. Jean Jacques is the object of attention,
and ridicule throws him like a fool
from his solitude. Well done.

A battered lamp, the day goes cadging,
and depends
like an asterisk mendicating
for itself maybe what emendations.

Now that the rain shines so pretty
in this one-lined peace,
here you have me,
here you have me, sun I depend on,
please sate my corners.

And if, when they're filled,
you overflow with greater goodness,
I'll draw from where there's nothing,
I'll forge in madness other basins,
insatiable desires
for level and love.

If then we go out ever to meet
what comes in the other side,
now, rainshone eternal and all,
here I am, sun I depend on,
I'm on the line. Here I am!

XXXI

Esperanza plañe entre algodones.

Aristas roncas uniformadas
de amenazas tejidas de esporas magníficas
y con porteros botones innatos.
¿Se luden seis de sol?
Natividad. Cállate, miedo.

Cristiano espero, espero siempre
de hinojos en la piedra circular que está
en las cien esquinas de esta suerte
tan vaga a donde asomo.

Y Dios sobresaltado nos oprime
el pulse, grave, mudo,
y como padre a su pequeña,
      apenas,
pero apenas, entreabre los sangrientos algodones
y entre sus dedos toma a la esperanza.

Señor, lo quiero yo . . .
Y basta!

XXXIV

Se acabó el extraño, con quien, tarde
la noche, regresabas parla y parla.
Ya no habrá quien me aguarde,
dispuesto mi lugar, bueno lo malo.

Se acabó la calurosa tarde;
tu, gran bahía y tu clamor; la charla
con tu madre acabada
que nos brindaba un té lleno de tarde.

XXXI

Hope mourns among the cotton.

Hoarse husks uniform
in menaces woven of magnificent spores
and with inborn porter's buttons.
Six of sun are chafing?
Nativity. Dread, be still.

Christian I hope, wait always
on my knees on the circular stone which is
at the hundred corners of this so vague
lot where I materialize.

And God astonished, presses our
pulse, grave, mute,
and like a father with his little girl,
        scarcely,
but scarcely, parts the bloodied cotton
and with his fingers picks out hope.

Señor, *I* want it ...
And that's enough!

XXXIV

Done with the stranger with whom, late
at night, you'd return in easy talk.
No-one waiting for me now,
my place arranged, good the bad.

Done with the hot afternoon;
your great bay and your clamour; the chatting
with your mother finished,
she would offer us tea full of afternoon.

Se acabó todo al fin: las vacaciones,
tu obediencia de pechos, tu manera
de pedirme que no me vaya fuera.

Y se acabó el diminutivo, para
mi mayoría en el dolor sin fin
y nuestro haber nacido así sin causa.

XXXVI

Pugnamos ensartamos por un ojo de aguja,
enfrentados, a las ganadas.
Amoniácase casi el cuarto ángulo del círculo.
¡Hembra se continúa el macho, a raíz
de probables senos, y precisamente
a raíz de cuanto no florece!

¿Por ahí estás, Venus de Milo?
Tú manqueas apenas pululando
entrañada en los brazos plenarios
de la existencia,
de esta existencia que todaviiza
perenne imperfección.
Venus de Milo, cuyo cercenado, increado
brazo revuélvese y trata de encodarse
a través de verdeantes guijarros gagos,
ortivos nautilos, aunes que gatean
recién, vísperas inmortales.
Laceadora de inminencias, laceadora
del paréntesis.

Rehusad, y vosotros, a posar las plantas
en la seguridad dupla de la Armonía.
Rehusad la simetría a buen seguro.
Intervenid en el conflicto
de puntas que se disputan

Done with everything at last: the holidays,
your breast obedience, your way
of asking me not to go away.

And done with the diminutive, for
my maturity in pain without end
and our having been born thus with no cause.

XXXVI

We are matched with ourselves, thread to the eye of a needle,
face on, out to win.
The fourth angle of the circle almost revives.
The male continues as female, by virtue
of probable breasts, and precisely
by virtue of all that does not flourish!

Are you here, Venus de Milo?
You are hardly maimed swarming
down deep in the full arms
of existence,
of this existence which
perennial imperfection yets.
Venus de Milo, whose severed, uncreated
arm turns and tries to make an elbow
across green stammering pebbles,
orient argonauts, perpetuals that go
newborn, deathless eves.
She, lassoer of imminences, lasher
of the parenthesis.

Refuse, you too, to place your soles
on the double security of Harmony.
Refuse trusty symmetry.
Intervene in the clash
of points in conflict

en la más torionda de las justas
el salto por el ojo de la aguja!

Tal siento ahora al meñique
demás en la siniestra. Lo veo y creo
no debe serme, o por lo menos que está
en sitio donde no debe.
Y me inspira rabia y me azarea
y no hay cómo salir de él, sino haciendo
la cuenta de que hoy es jueves.

¡Ceded al nuevo impar
                    potente de orfandad!

XLI

La Muerte de rodillas mana
su sangre blanca que no es sangre.
Se huele a garantía.
Pero ya me quiero reír.

Murmúrase algo por allí. Callan.
Alguien silba valor de lado,
y hasta se contaría en par
veintitrés costillas que se echan de menos
entre sí, a ambos costados; se contaría
en par también, toda la fila
de trapecios escoltas.

En tanto, el redoblante policial
(otra vez me quiero reír)
se desquita y nos tunde a palos,
dale y dale,
de membrana a membrana
tas
con
tas.

in the most ruttish of jousts
the leap through the eye of the needle!

So now I feel my little finger
superfluous on my left hand. I see it and think
it shouldn't be mine, or at least that it's
somewhere it shouldn't be.
And it enrages and perplexes me
and there's no way out of it, except
by reckoning that today is Thursday.

Make way for the new masculine number
mighty in orphanhood!

XLI

Death kneeling oozes
her white blood which is not blood.
Smell of guarantee.
But now I want to laugh.

They're murmuring something over there. Silence.
Someone whistles pluck obliquely,
and there could even be a paired count of
twenty-three ribs which regret each others'
absence, on both sides; a count
in pairs also, of the whole file
of accessory trapezes.

Meanwhile the police drummer
(again I want to laugh)
retaliates and mugs us,
applies his stick,
from skin to skin
whack
on
whack.

LVI

Todos los días amanezco a ciegas
a trabajar para vivir; y tomo el desayuno,
sin probar ni gota de él, todas las mañanas.
Sin saber si he logrado, o más nunca,
algo que brinca del sabor
o es sólo corazón y que ya vuelto, lamentará
hasta dónde esto es lo menos.

El niño crecería ahito de felicidad
          oh albas,
ante el pesar de los padres de no poder dejarnos
de arrancar de sus sueños de amor a este mundo;
ante ellos que, como Dios, de tanto amor
se comprendieron hasta creadores
y nos quisieron hasta hacernos daño.

Flecos de invisible trama,
dientes que huronean desde la neutra emoción,
          pilares
libres de base y coronación,
en la gran boca que ha perdido el habla.

Fósforo y fósforo en la oscuridad,
lágrima y lágrima en la polvareda.

LVII

Craterizados los puntos más altos, los puntos
del amor de ser mayúsculo, bebo, ayuno, ab-
sorbo heroína para la pena, para el latido
lacio y contra toda corrección.

¿Puedo decir que nos han traicionado? No.
¿Que todos fueron buenos? Tampoco. Pero

LVI

Every day I rise blindly
to work to live: and I have breakfast
not tasting a drop of it, every morning.
Not knowing if I have made it, or ever shall,
something that leaps out from the taste
or is only heart, something come back that will lament
until this is the least thing here.

Children would grow up sated with happiness
        oh bright morning,
before the sorrow of our parents unable to leave us unable
to escape their dreams of love for this world;
like God so full with love
they thought themselves creators
loved us with warm injury.

Ornate edges of invisible weft
teeth that hunt with a ferret from a blind of neuter emotions
        columns
of no base no coronation,
in the huge speechlost mouth.

Match after match in the dark,
tear after tear in a cloud of dust.

LVII

The highest points are cratered, the points
of the love of being the first letter, I drink, I fast, I sho–
ot heroin into the grief, straight
into the lank throb and against all correction.

Can I say they have betrayed us? No.
That they were all good? No again. But

allí está una buena voluntad, sin duda,
y sobre todo, el ser así.

¡Y qué quien se ame mucho! Yo me busco
en mi propio designio que debió ser obra
mía, en vano: nada alcanzó a ser libre.

Y sin embargo, quién me empuja.
A que no me atrevo a cerrar la quinta ventana.
Y el papel de amarse y persistir, junto a las
horas y a lo indebido.

Y el éste y el aquél.

LX

Es de madera mi paciencia,
    sorda vejetal.

Día que has sido puro, niño, inútil,
que naciste desnudo, las leguas
de tu marcha, van corriendo sobre
tus doce extremidades, ese doblez ceñudo
que después deshiláchase
en no se sabe qué últimos pañales.

Constelado de hemisferios de grumo,
bajo eternas américas inéditas, tu gran plumaje,
te partes y me dejas, sin tu emoción ambigua
sin tu nudo de sueños, domingo.

Y se apolilla mi paciencia,
y me vuelvo a exclamar: ¡Cuándo vendrá
el domingo bocón y mudo del sepulcro;
cuándo vendrá a cargar este sábado
de harapos, esta horrible sutura

a willingness exists there, without doubt,
and above all, that's how it is.

And what if you love yourself very much! I search for me
in my own design which ought to have been my own
work, in vain: nothing gained by being free.

All the same, who is pushing me.
To the point I don't dare close the fifth window.
And the act of loving the self and persisting, up against
the hours and the wrongness.

The man is Everywhere.

LX

Of wood is my patience,
silent vegetable.

Day, you have been pure, a child, useless,
born naked, the leagues
of your path, go running along
your twelve extremities, this grimbrowed folding
which later comes apart
into it isn't known what final infancies.

Constellated from hemispheres of clot
under eternal unknown americas, your great plumage,
you dispatch yourself and leave me, without your ambiguous
    emotion
without your tangle of dreams, Sunday.

And my patience becomes worm eaten
and I turn to speak out: when will
come mute Sunday opening in the tomb,
when come to load up this Saturday

del placer que nos engendra sin querer,
y el placer que nos DestieRRa!

LXIX

Qué nos buscas, oh mar, con tus volúmenes
docentes! Qué inconsolable, qué atroz
estás en la febril solana.

Con tus azadones saltas,
con tus hojas saltas,
hachando, hachando en loco sésamo,
mientras tornan llorando las olas, después
de descalcar los cuatro vientos
y todos los recuerdos, en labiados plateles
de tungsteno, contractos de colmillos
y estáticas eles quelonias.

Filosofía de alas negras que vibran
al medroso temblor de los hombros del día.

El mar, y una edición en pie,
en su única hoja el anverso
de cara al reverso.

LXXVII

Graniza tanto, como para que yo recuerde
y acreciente las perlas
que he recogido del hocico mismo
de cada tempestad.

No se vaya a secar esta lluvia.
A menos que me fuese dado

of rags, this horrible suture
of the pleasure which begets us unwillingly,
and the pleasure which IsoLates us.

LXIX

How you hunt us, oh sea with your doctrinal
volumes. How inconsolable, how enormous
you are in the fevered sun-haunt.

With your adze you 'sault,
with your blade you 'sault,
slashing, slashing in mad sesame,
while the waves turn weeping, after
uncaulking the four winds
and all memorabilia, in edged platters
of tungsten, canine contractions
and ecstatic chelonian Ls.

Philosophy of black wings that vibrate
to the timid quaking of the day's shoulders.
The sea, and an edition established,
on its one page the reverse
faced by the obverse.

LXXVII

It hails so much, as if I should recall
and increase the pearls
I've gathered from the very snout
of every storm.

This rain must not dry.
Unless now I could fall

caer ahora para ella, o que me enterrasen
mojado en el agua
que surtiera de todos los fuegos.

¿Hasta dónde me alcanzará esta lluvia?
Temo me quede con algún flanco seco;
temo que ella se vaya, sin haberme probado
en las sequías de increíbles cuerdas vocales,
por las que
para dar armonía,
hay siempre que subir ¡nunca bajar!
¿No subimos acaso para abajo?

¡Canta, lluvia, en la costa aún sin mar!

in her cause, or were buried
steeped in the water
which spouts from all fires.

How much will this rain get to me?
I fear I am left with a flank dry;
I fear it might break leaving me untried
in the drought of incredible vocal chords,
over which
to bring harmony
one must always rise, never descend!
Do we not rise downwards?

Sing, rain, on the coast still without sea!

POEMAS HUMANOS

Voy a hablar de la esperanza

Yo no sufro este dolor como César Vallejo. Yo no me duelo ahora como artista, como hombre ni como simple ser vivo siquiera. Yo no sufro este dolor como católico, como mahometano ni como ateo. Hoy sufro solamente. Si no me llamase César Vallejo, también sufriría este mismo dolor. Si no fuese artista, también lo sufriría. Si no fuese hombre ni ser vivo siquiera, también lo sufriría. Si no fuese católico, ateo ni mahometano, también lo sufriría. Hoy sufro desde más abajo. Hoy sufro solamente. Me duelo ahora sin explicaciones. Mi dolor es tan hondo, que no tuvo ya causa ni carece de causa.

¿Qué sería su causa? ¿Dónde está aquello tan importante, que dejase de ser su causa? Nada es su causa; nada ha podido dejar de ser su causa. ¿A qué ha nacido este dolor, por sí mismo? Mi dolor es del viento del norte y del viento del sur, como esos huevos neutros que algunas aves raras ponen del viento. Si hubiera muerto mi novia, mi dolor sería igual. Si me hubieran cortado el cuello de raíz, mi dolor sería igual. Si la vida fuese, en fin, de otro modo, mi dolor sería igual. Hoy sufro desde más arriba. Hoy sufro solamente.

Miro el dolor del hambriento y veo que su hambre anda tan lejos de mi sufrimiento, que de quedarme ayuno hasta morir, saldría siempre de mi tumba una brizna de yerba al menos. Lo mismo el enamorado. ¡Qué sangre la suya más engendrada, para la mía sin fuente ni consumo!

Yo creía hasta ahora que todas las cosas del universo eran, inevitablemente, padres o hijos. Pero he aquí que mi dolor de hoy no es padre ni es hijo. Le falta espalda para anochecer, tanto como le sobra pecho para amanecer y si lo pusiesen en una estancia oscura, no daría luz y si lo pusiesen en una estancia luminosa, no echaría sombra. Hoy sufro suceda lo que suceda. Hoy sufro solamente.

HUMAN POEMS

I'm going to talk about hope

It isn't as César Vallejo that I suffer this pain. I do not ache as an artist, as a man or even because I'm simply alive. I don't suffer this pain as a Catholic, Mohammedan, or atheist. Today my suffering has no attribution. If I were not César Vallejo, I should suffer this pain no less. If I weren't an artist, no less. If I weren't a man or even a live thing, no less. If I were not a Catholic, atheist, or Mohammedan, the suffering would go on. Today I suffer from deeper down. Today I suffer purely.

There is no explanation for my hurting. It is so deep it had no cause nor does it lack cause. What could be the cause? What is so important that it could cease to be the cause? Nothing is the cause of it. Nothing could refuse to be the cause. For what was this pain born, for itself? My wound is from the northwind and from the southwind, like those genderless eggs rare birds lay on the wind. If my sweetheart had died, no difference. If they had cut off my neck at the root, all the same. If life in fact was otherwise, my pain would not change. Today I suffer from another place. Today I suffer purely.

I look at the hungry man and see that where his hunger works is so far short of my suffering that were I to fast until I died a shoot would still always emerge from my tomb. The same with the man in love. His swollen blood compared to mine is fountainless and unconsummated!

Until now I thought all things in the universe were inevitably fathers or sons. But now I see my pain today is neither father nor son. It has too little foundation to grow dark and it has too much appearance for rising, and if they put it in a dark room, it would give no light and if they put it in a bright room, it would cast no shadow. Today I suffer whatever is there. Today I suffer purely.

Me estoy riendo

Un guijarro, uno solo, el más bajo de todos,
controla
a todo el médano aciago y faraónico.

El aire adquiere tensión de recuerdo y de anhelo,
y bajo el sol se calla
hasta exigir el cuello a las pirámides.

Sed. Hidratada melancolía de la tribu errabunda,
gota
a
gota,
del siglo al minuto.

Son tres Treses paralelos,
barbados de barba inmemorial,
en marcha   3   3   3

Es el tiempo este anuncio de gran zapatería,
es el tiempo, que marcha descalzo
de la muerte   hacia   la   muerte.

epístola a los transeúntes

Reanudo mi día de conejo,
mi noche de elefante en descanso.

Y, entre mí, digo:
ésta mi inmensidad en bruto, a cántaros,
éste mi grato peso, que me buscara abajo para pájaro;
éste es mi brazo
que por su cuenta rehusó ser ala,

I'm laughing

A pebble, one alone, the lowest of them all,
controls
the whole foreboding, pharaonic dune.

The air acquires tension of memory and yearning,
and under the sun falls quiet
until it exacts from the pyramids their neck.

Thirst. Hydrated melancholy of the wandering tribe,
drop
by
drop,
from the century to the minute.

There are three Threes parallel,
bearded men of immemorial beard,
marching   3   3   3

This is the time of the great shoestore ad,
is the time which marches barefoot
from death   towards   death.

epistle to the transients

I resume my rabbit day,
my fallow elephant night.

And within myself, I say:
this is my hugeness raw, by buckets,
this is my welcome weight which sought me below for finch;
this is my arm
which of its own accord spurned the wing;

éstas son mis sagradas escrituras,
éstos mis alarmados compañones.

Lúgubre isla me alumbrará continental,
mientras el capitolio se apoye en mi íntimo derrumbe
y la asamblea en lanzas clausure mi desfile.

Pero cuando yo muera
de vida y no de tiempo,
cuando lleguen a dos mis dos maletas,
éste ha de ser mi estómago en que cupo mi lámpara en pedazos,
ésta aquella cabeza que expió los tormentos del círculo en mis pasos,
éstos esos gusanos que el corazón contó por unidades,
éste ha de ser mi cuerpo solidario
por el que vela el alma individual; éste ha de ser
mi hombligo en que maté mis piojos natos,
ésta mi cosa cosa, mi cosa tremebunda.

En tanto, convulsiva, ásperamente
convalece mi freno,
sufriendo como sufro del lenguaje directo del léon;
y, puesto que he existido entre dos potestades de ladrillo,
convalezco yo mismo, sonriendo de mis labios.

Los nueve monstruos

I, desgraciadamente,
el dolor crece en el mundo a cada rato,
crece a treinta minutos por segundo, paso a paso,
y la naturaleza del dolor, es el dolor dos veces
y la condición del martirio, carnívora, voraz,
es el dolor dos veces
y la función de la yerba purísima, el dolor
dos veces
y el bien de sér, dolernos doblemente.

these are my sacred scriptures,
these my testy twosome.

Gothick isle will illumine me, continental,
while the capitol leans on my private collapse
and the assembly in spears closes my parade.

But when I die
of life and not of time,
when my two suitcases make 2,
this shall be my stomach, container of a shattered lamp,
this head the one which bore the circle torture in my steps,
these worms the ones my heart counted in units,
this shall be my solidary body
tended by an individual soul; this shall be
my navel where I killed my inherent lice,
this my thing thing, my dreadful thing.

Meanwhile, convulsive, harshly
my rein recovers,
suffering as I suffer from the lion's direct idiom;
and since I have existed between two potentates of brick
I myself recover, smiling with my lips.

The nine monsters

And unfortunately,
pain grows in the world every moment,
grows at thirty minutes a second, step by step,
and the nature of pain is pain twice
and the condition of the martyrdom, flesh-eating, voracious,
is pain twice
and the function of the purest grass, pain
twice
and the good of being, to hurt us doubly.

Jamás, hombres humanos,
hubo tanto dolor en el pecho, en la solapa, en la cartera,
en el vaso, en la carnicería, en la aritmética!
Jamás tanto cariño doloroso,
jamás tan cerca arremetió lo lejos,
jamás el fuego nunca
jugó mejor su rol de frío muerto!
Jamás, señor ministro de salud, fue la salud
más mortal
y la migrana extrajo tanta frente de la frente!
Y el mueble tuvo en su cajón, dolor,
el corazón, en su cajón, dolor,
la lagartija, en su cajón, dolor.

Crece la desdicha, hermanos hombres,
más pronto que la máquina, a diez máquinas, y crece
con la res de Rousseau, con nuestras barbas;
crece el mal por razones que ignoramos
y es una inundación con propios líquidos,
con propio barro y propia nube sólida!
Invierte el sufrimiento posiciones, da función
en que el humor acuoso es vertical
al pavimento,
el ojo es visto y esta oreja oída,
y esta oreja da nueve campanadas a la hora
del rayo, y nueve carcajadas
a la hora del trigo, y nueve sones hembras
a la hora del llanto, y nueve cánticos
a la hora del hambre, y nueve truenos
y nueve látigos, menos un grito.

El dolor nos agarra, hermanos hombres,
por detrás, de perfil,
y nos aloca en los cinemas,
nos clava en los gramófonos,
nos desclava en los lechos, cae perpendicularmente
a nuestros boletos, a nuestras cartas;

Never, human men,
was there so much pain in the chest, in the lapel, in the wallet,
in the glass, in the butcher's, in arithmetic!
Never so much painful affection,
never did so near charge the far,
never did fire ever
better play its part as dead fire!
Never, Minister of Health, was health
more mortal
did migraine extract so much brow from the brow!
And the furniture had in its drawer, pain,
the heart in its drawer, pain,
the lizard in its drawer, pain.

Distress grows, brother men,
faster than the engine, at ten engines, and grows
with Rousseau's stock, with our beards;
evil grows for reasons we don't know
it's a flood with its own liquids,
its own mud and its own solid cloud.
Suffering inverts positions, in a geometry
where the aqueous humour stands per-
pendicular,
the eye is seen and this ear, heard,
and this car tolls nine at the hour
of discharge, nine guffaws
at the hour of wheat, and nine female sounds
at the hour of weeping, and nine canticles
at the hour of hunger, and nine thunderclaps
 and nine lashes, minus one shout.

Pain grabs us, brother men,
flora behind, in profile,
crazes us in cinemas,
nails us to gramophones,
un-nails us to beds, falls vertically
to our tickets, our letters;

y es muy grave sufrir, puede uno orar ...
Pues de resultas
del dolor, hay algunos
que nacen, otros crecen, otros mueren,
y otros que nacen y no mueren, otros
que sin haber nacido, mueren, y otros
que no nacen ni mueren (son los más).
Y también de resultas
del sufrimiento, estoy triste
hasta la cabeza, y más triste hasta el tobillo,
de ver al pan, crucificado, al nabo,
ensangrentado,
llorando, a la cebolla,
al cereal, en general, harina,
a la sal, hecha polvo, al agua, huyendo,
al vino, un ecce-homo,
tan pálida a la nieve, al sol tan ardio!
¡Cómo, hermanos humanos,
no deciros que ya no puedo y
ya no puedo con tanto cajón,
tanto minuto, tanta
lagartija y tanta
inversión, tanto lejos y tanta sed de sed!
Señor Ministro de Salud: ¿qué hacer?
¡Ah! desgraciadamente, hombres humanos,
hay, hermanos, muchísimo que hacer.

Va corriendo, andando ...

Va corriendo, andando, huyendo
de sus pies ...
Va con dos nubes en su nube,
sentado apócrifo, en la mano insertos
sus tristes paras, sus entonces fúnebres.

suffering is serious, one might pray ...
For as a result
of pain, there are some
who are born, others grow, others die,
and others who are born and don't die, others
who die unborn, and others
who neither are born nor die (most).
And also as a result
of suffering I'm sad
up to my head, and sadder down to my ankle,
seeing bread crucified, the turnip
bloodied,
the onion weeping,
cereal in general as flour,
salt ground to dust, water fleeing,
wine as an ecce-homo,
snow so pale, the sun so scorched!
How, human brothers,
not to tell you I can no longer and
I can no longer stand so much drawer,
so much minute, so much
lizard and so much
inversion, so much distance and such thirst for thirst!
Minister of Health: what is to be done ?
Unfortunately, human men,
brothers, there is so much to be done.

He goes running, walking ...

He goes running, walking, flying
from his feet ...
He goes with two clouds on his cloud,
in apocryphal attire, his sad wherefores
his glum therefores inserted in his hand.

Corre de todo, andando
entre protestas incoloras; huye
subiendo, huye
bajando, huye
a paso de sotana, huye
alzando al mal en brazos,
huye,
directamente a sollozar a solas.

Adonde vaya,
lejos de sus fragosos, cáusticos talones,
lejos del aire, lejos de su viaje,
a fin de huir, huir y huir y huir
de sus pies—hombre en dos pies, parado
de tanto huir—habrá sed de correr.

¡Y ni el árbol, si endosa hierro de oro!
¡Y ni el hierro, si cubre su hojarasca!
Nada, sino sus pies,
nada sino su breve calofrío,
sus paras vivos, sus entonces vivos ...

Piedra negra sobre una piedra blanca

Me moriré en París con aguacero,
un día del cual tengo ya el recuerdo.
Me moriré en París—y no me corro—
talvez un jueves, como es hoy, de otoño.

Jueves será, porque hoy, jueves, que proso
estos versos, los húmeros me he puesto
a la mala y, jamás como hoy, me he vuelto,
con todo mi camino, a verme solo.

Away from everything he runs, moving
between colourless protests; he flies
rising, he flies
descending, he flies
with the cassock's passing, he flies
bearing evil in his arms,
flies
straight away to weep alone.

Wherever he goes,
far from his rough caustic heels,
far from the wind, far from his journey,
his purpose to fly and fly and fly
from his feet—man on two feet, checked
from so much flight—will have a thirst for running.

And not the tree, if iron is endorsed with gold!
And not iron, if its old leaves are covered!
Nothing, but his feet,
nothing but his brief chill,
his living wherefores, his living therefores . . .

Black stone on a white stone

I shall die in Paris in heavy rain
the day is entered in my brain
I shall die in Paris—and that's a promise—
maybe some Thursday, like this one, in autumn.

Thursday for sure, this Thursday when I churn
these verses, I've placed my arms
with bad grace and never as today have I turned
with my whole load, to see myself alone.

César Vallejo ha muerto, le pegaban
todos sin que él les haga nada;
le daban duro con un palo y duro

también con una soga; son testigos
los días jueves y los huesos húmeros,
la soledad, la lluvia, los caminos ...

Intensidad y altura

Quiero escribir, pero me sale espuma,
quiero decir muchísimo y me atollo;
no hay cifra hablada que no sea suma,
no hay pirámide escrita, sin cogollo.

Quiero escribir, pero me siento puma;
quiero laurearme, pero me encebollo.
No hay toz hablada, que no llegue a bruma,
no hay dios ni hijo de dios, sin desarrollo.

Vámonos, pues, por eso, a comer yerba,
carne de llanto, fruta de gemido,
nuestra alma melancólica en conserva.

Vámonos! Vámonos! Estoy herido;
Vámonos a beber lo ya bebido,
vámonos, cuervo, a fecundar tu cuerva.

Acaba de pasar ...

Acaba de pasar el que vendrá
proscrito, a sentarse en mi triple desarrollo;
acaba de pasar criminalmente.

César Vallejo is dead, they nailed him down
everyone did, though he did nothing
they hit him heavy with sticks and heavy

with a rope; for witnesses are
the Thursdays, these armbones,
the aloneness, the rain, the road ...

Intensity and height

I want to write, but out comes foam,
I want to speak and I'm stuck inside;
There's no number spoken that isn't a sum
There's no writ pyramid without seed.

I want to write but I sense the puma:
I want to be laureate, but make a stew with onion
There's no spoken word unequal to weather
there's no god or son without extension.

Come on then, let's go eat clover,
weeping flesh, fruit of displeasure
our injured soul prepared for store.

Come on, come on! I've got enough to suffer
Let's go to drink what's already measure,
come on my crow, let's go to your lover.

He who will come ...

He who will come has just gone by
denounced, and settled himself on my triple unfolding;
he has just gone by like a criminal.

Acaba de sentarse más acá,
a un cuerpo de distancia de mi alma,
el que vino en un asno a enflaquecerme;
acaba de sentarse de pie, lívido.

Acaba de darme lo que está acabado,
el calor del fuego y el pronombre inmenso
que el animal crió bajo su cola.

Acaba
de expresarme su duda sobre hipótesis lejanas
que él aleja, aún más, con la mirada.

Acaba de hacer al bien los honores que le tocan
en virtud del infame paquidermo,
por lo soñado en mí y en él matado.

Acaba de ponerme (no hay primera)
su segunda aflixión en plenos lomos
y su tercer sudor en plena lágrima.

Acaba de pasar sin haber venido.

La rueda del hambriento

Por entre mis propios dientes salgo humeando,
dando voces, pujando,
bajándome los pantalones ...
Váca mi estómago, váca mi yeyuno,
la miseria me saca por entre mis propios dientes,
cogido con un palito por el puño de la camisa.

Una piedra en que sentarme
¿no habrá ahora para mí?
Aun aquella piedra en que tropieza la mujer que ha dado a luz,

He has just come down,
a body of distance from my soul,
the man who came on a cuddy to weaken me;
he has just planted himself, livid.

He has just given me that which is finished,
the heat of the fire and the immense pronoun
which the animal reared under its tail.

He has just
expressed to me his doubts on distant hypotheses
which he repels still further with his gaze.

He has just done to good,
infamous pachyderm, honours there due,
because of what in me is dreamt and in him killed.

He has just placed (there's no first)
his second affliction full on my back
and his third sweat full in my tear.

He has just gone by having never come.

The hungry man's rack

Out through my own teeth I go fuming,
shouting, pushing,
dropping my pants ...
My stomach vacates, my jejunum vacates,
lack pulls me out through my own teeth,
caught with a toothpick by my shirtcuff.

Has anybody got a stone
I can sit down on now?
Even that stone which balks the woman who has given birth,

la madre del cordero, la causa, la raíz,
¿ésa no habrá ahora para mí?
¡Siquiera aquella otra,
que ha pasado agachándose por mi alma!
Siquiera
la calcárida o la mala (humilde océano)
o la que ya no sirve ni para ser tirada contra el hombre,
¡ésa dádmela ahora para mí!

Siquiera la que hallaren atravesada y sola en un insulto,
¡ésa dádmela ahora para mí!
Siquiera la torcida y coronada, en que resuena
solamente una vez el andar de las rectas conciencias,
o, al menos, esa otra, que arrojada en digna curva,
va a caer por sí misma,
en profesión de entraña verdadera,
¡ésa dádmela ahora para mí!

Un pedazo de pan, ¿tampoco habrá ahora para mí?
Ya no más he de ser lo que siempre he de ser,
pero dadme
una piedra en que sentarme,
pero dadme,
por favor, un pedazo de pan en que sentarme,
pero dadme
en español
algo, en fin de beber, de comer, de vivir, de reposarse,
y después me iré ...
Hallo una extraña forma, está muy rota
y sucia mi camisa
y ya no tengo nada, esto es horrendo.

the mother of the lamb, the cause, the root,
is there such a stone for me?
At least that other stone,
which has gone cowering through my soul!
At least
the calcar or the bad one (humble ocean)
or the one you'd not even throw at man,
give it to me now!

Or else the one they find pierced and alone in an insult,
give that one to me now!
Even a twisted and crowned one, on which resounds
but once the tread of upright consciences,
or if nothing else, that other one which thrown in a worthy arc,
is about to fall of itself,
professing a true entrail,
give it to me now!

Has nobody got a piece of bread for me, either?
I shall no longer be what I shall always be,
but give me,
a stone to sit on,
but give me
please, a piece of bread to sit on,
but give me
in Spanish
something, finally, to drink, to eat, to live, to rest,
and then I'll go away ...
I find a strange shape, my shirt is
dirty and in shreds
and I've got nothing left, this is hideous

Palmas y guitarra

Ahora, entre nosotros, aquí,
ven conmigo, trae por la mano a tu cuerpo
y cenemos juntos y pasemos un instante la vida
a dos vidas y dando una parte a nuestra muerte.
Ahora, ven contigo, hazme el favor
de quejarte en mi nombre y a la luz de la noche teneblosa
en que traes a tu alma de la mano
y huimos en puntillas de nosotros.

Ven a mí, sí, y a ti, sí,
con paso par, a vernos a los dos con paso impar,
marcar el paso de la despedida.
¡Hasta cuando volvamos! ¡Hasta la vuelta!
¡Hasta cuando leamos, ignorantes!
¡Hasta cuando volvamos, despidámonos!

¿Qué me importan los fusiles,
escúchame;
escúchame, qué impórtanme,
si la bala circula ya en el rango de mi firma?
¿Qué te importan a ti las balas,
si el fusil está humeando ya en tu olor?
Hoy mismo pesaremos
en los brazos de un ciego nuestra estrella
y, una vez que me cantes, lloraremos.
Hoy mismo, hermosa, con tu paso par
y tu confianza a que llegó mi alarma,
saldremos de nosotros, dos a dos.
¡Hasta cuando seamos ciegos!
¡Hasta
que lloremos de tanto volver!

Ahora,
entre nosotros, trae
por la mano a tu dulce personaje

Palms and guitar

Now, between ourselves, here,
come with me, bring your body by the hand
and we'll sup together and pass life for an instant
to two lives giving a share to our death.
Now, come with you, do me the favour
of complaining in my name in the light of the tenebrous night
in which you bring your soul by the hand
and we fly softly from ourselves.

Come to me, and to you, yes,
with even step, to see both of us with uneven step,
marking the final pass.
Till we come back! Till next time!
Till we read, ignorantes!
Till we come back, let's say goodbye!

What are guns to me,
listen;
listen to me, what are they
when the bullet already travels my signature's rank?
What are bullets to you
when the gun is already smoking in your scent?
This very day we'll weigh
our star in a blind man's arms
and once you sing for me we shall weep.
This same day, beautiful girl, with your even step
and your courage sounded by my alarm,
we'll issue from ourselves, two by two.
Until we're blind!
Till
we weep from such returning!

Now,
between ourselves, bring
your gentle person by the hand

y cenemos juntos y pasemos un instante la vida
a dos vidas y dando una parte a nuestra muerte.
Ahora, ven contigo, hazme el favor
de cantar algo
y de tocar en tu alma, haciendo palmas.
¡Hasta cuando volvamos! ¡Hasta entonces!
¡Hasta cuando partamos, despidámonos!

París, octubre 1936

De todo esto yo soy el único que parte.
De este banco me voy, de mis calzones,
de mi gran situación, de mis acciones,
de mi número hendido parte a parte,
de todo esto yo soy el único que parte.

De los Campos Elíseos o al dar vuelta
la extraña callejuela de la Luna,
mi defunción se va, parte mi cuna,
y, rodeada de gente, sola, suelta,
mi semejanza humana dase vuelta
y despacha sus sombras una a una.

Y me alejo de todo, porque todo
se queda para hacer la coartada:
mi zapato, su ojal, también su lodo
y hasta el doblez del codo
de mi propia camisa abotonada.

and we'll sup together and pass life for an instant
to two lives giving a share to our death.
Now, come with you, do me the favour
of singing something
of playing on your soul, clapping palms.
Till we come back! Till then!
Until we part, let's say goodbye!

Paris, October 1936

From this whole thing I'm the only one leaving
From this bank I'm going, from my trousers
from my great position, from my shares,
from my number, cleaved in two
from the whole thing I am the only one leaving

From the Champs Elysées or turning around
into the strange alley of the Moon,
my death goes down, my cradle goes on
and surrounded by people, solo, insulate
my human semblance rotates
and loosens its shades one by one

And I move away from all of it, because it
stays to provide the alibi:
my shoe, its eyelet, also its dirt
and even the elbow crease of my
own buttoned shirt.

Los desgraciados

Ya va a venir el día; da
cuerda a tu brazo, búscate debajo
del colchón, vuelve a pararte
en tu cabeza, para andar derecho
Ya va a venir el día, ponte el saco.

Ya va a venir el día; ten
fuerte en la mano a tu intestino grande, reflexiona
antes de meditar, pues es horrible
cuando le cae a uno la desgracia
y se le cae a uno a fondo el diente.

Necesitas comer, pero, me digo,
no tengas pena, que no es de pobres
la pena, el sollozar junto a su tumba;
remiéndate, recuerda,
confía en tu hilo blanco, fuma, pasa lista
a tu cadena y guárdala detrás de tu retrato.
Ya va a venir el día, ponte el alma.

Ya va a venir el día, pasan,
han abierto en el hotel un ojo,
azotándolo, dándole con un espejo tuyo ...
¿Tiemblas? Es el estado remoto de la frente
y la nación reciente del estómago.
Roncan aún! ... ¡Qué universo se lleva este ronquido!
¡Cómo quedan tus poros, enjuiciándolo!
¡Con cuántos doses ¡ay! estás tan solo!
Ya va a venir el día, ponte el sueño.

Ya va a venir el día, repito
por el órgano oral de tu silencio
y urge tomar la izquierda con el hambre
y tomar la derecha con la sed; de todos modos,
abstente de ser pobre con los ricos,

The unfortunates

The day is about to come; wind up
your arm, look for yourself under
the sheet, stand on your head
again and walk straight.
The day is about to come, put your jacket on.

The day is about to come; get
a firm hold on your colon, reflect
sooner than meditate, it's no good
when bad luck falls on you
and your tooth falls right out.

You need to eat, but I say to myself
don't feel sorry, for sorrow is inappropriate
to the poor, so is weeping by their tomb;
patch yourself up, remember,
trust in your white thread, smoke, check
your chain and put it behind your photograph.
The day is about to come, put your soul on.

The day is about to come; they go by,
they've opened an eye in the hotel,
lashing it, hitting it with a mirror of yours . . .
You're shaking? It's the remote state of your brow
and the recent nation of your stomach.
They're still snoring . . . What a universe that snore removed!
Your pores in this state, indicting it!
With so many twins you're so alone!
The day is about to come, put on your dream.

The day is about to come, I repeat
through the oral organ of your silence,
and mind you take the left with your hunger
and the right with your thirst; in any case,
refrain from being poor with the rich,

atiza
tu frío, porque en él se integra mi calor, amada víctima.
Ya va a venir el día, ponte el cuerpo.

Ya va a venir el día;
la mañana, la mar, el meteoro, van
en pos de tu cansancio, con banderas,
y, por tu orgullo clásico, las hienas
cuentan sus pasos al compás del asno,
la panadera piensa en ti,
el carnicero piensa en ti, palpando
el hacha en que están presos
el acero y el hierro y el metal; jamás olvides
que durante la misa no hay amigos.
Ya va a venir el día, ponte el sol.

Ya viene el día; dobla
el aliento, triplica
tu bondad rencorosa
y da codos al miedo, nexo y énfasis,
pues tú, como se observa en tu entrepierna y siendo
el malo ¡ay! inmortal,
has soñado esta noche que vivías
de nada y morías de todo ...

El acento me pende del zapato

El acento me pende del zapato;
le oigo perfectamente
sucumbir, lucir, doblarse en forma de ámbar
y colgar, colorante, mala sombra.
Me sobra así el tamaño,
me ven jueces desde un árbol,
me ven con sus espaldas ir de frente,
entrar a mi martillo,

poke
your cold, because my warmth is one with it, beloved victim.
The day is about to come, put on your body.

The day is about to come;
morning, main, meteorite process
behind your fatigue with banners,
and given your classic pride hyenas
count their steps to a donkey's rhythm,
the baker's girl thinks of you,
the butcher thinks of you, fondling
the cleaver that imprisons
steel and iron and metal; never forget
that during Mass friends are absent.
The day is about to come, put on your sun.

The day is about to come; double
your verve, triple
your rancorous goodness
and elbow out fear, nexus and emphasis,
for (as your middle leg shows, the-evil-one
being, alas, immortal) you
dreamt last night you lived
on nothing and died of every thing ...

The accent hangs from my shoe

The accent hangs from my shoe;
I hear him perfectly
succumb, shine, bend in amber form
and hang on, a coloration, a bad shade.
This way I'm oversize,
judges see me from a tree,
via their backs they see me go forward
into my hammer,

pararme a ver a una niña
y, al pie de un urinario, alzar los hombros.

Seguramente nadie está a mi lado,
me importa poco, no lo necesito;
seguramente han dicho que me vaya:
lo siento claramente.

¡Cruelísimo tamaño el de rezar!
¡Humillación, fulgor, profunda selva!
Me sobra ya tamaño, bruma elástica,
rapidez por encima y desde y junto.
¡Imperturbable! ¡Imperturbable! Suenan
luego, después, fatídicos teléfonos.
Es el acento: es él.

Quiere y no quiere ...

Quiere y no quiere su color mi pecho,
por cuyas bruscas vías voy, lloro con palo,
trato de ser feliz, lloro en mi mano,
recuerdo, escribo
y remacho una lágrima en mi pómulo.

Quiere su rojo el mal, el bien su rojo enrojecido
por el hacha suspensa,
por el trote del ala a pie volando,
y no quiere y sensiblemente
no quiere aquesto el hombre;
no quiere estar en su alma
acostado, en la sien latidos de asta,
el bimano, el muy bruto, el muy filósofo.

Así, casi no soy, me vengo abajo
desde el arado en que socorro a mi alma

stop to see a little girl
and, at the urinal, shrug my shoulders.

Certainly nobody's at my side.
I don't care much, I don't need it;
certainly they've said I should go:
I feel it clearly.

The cruellest size is when you're praying!
Humiliation, flare, deep forest!
I am oversize, elastic fog,
quickness above and from and by.
Imperturbable! Imperturbable! Immediately then
prophetic telephones ring.
It's the accent; it's him.

My heart will and won't have its hue

My heart will and won't have its hue,
through those brusque tracts I go, weep with a splint,
try to be happy, weep in my hand,
remember, write
and clinch a tear on my cheek-bone.

Evil will have its red, goodness its red reddened
by the poised axe,
by the trot of the wing flying afoot,
and man won't have
palpably will not have that;
won't be couched
in his soul, horn-throbs in his temple,
bimane, most brutish, the great philosopher.

Thus, I almost am not, I come tumbling
from the plough that succours my soul

y casi, en proporción, casi enaltézcome.
Que saber por qué tiene la vida este perrazo,
por qué lloro, por qué,
cejón, inhábil, veleidoso, hube nacido
gritado;
saberlo, comprenderlo
al son de un alfabeto competente,
sería padecer por un ingrato.

¡Y no! ¡No! ¡No! ¡Qué ardid, ni paramento!
Congoja, sí, con sí firme y frenético,
coriáceo, rapaz, quiere y no quiere, cielo y pájaro;
congoja, sí, con toda la bragueta.
Contienda entre dos llantos, robo de una sola ventura,
vía indolora en que padezco en chanclos
de la velocidad de andar a ciegas.

Marcha nupcial

A la cabeza de mis propios actos,
corona en mano, batallón de dioses,
el signo negativo al cuello, atroces
el fósforo y la prisa, estupefactos
el alma y el valor, con dos impactos

al pie de la mirada; dando voces;
los límites, dinámicos, feroces;
tragándome los lloros inexactos;

me encenderé, se encenderá mi hormiga,
se encenderán mi llave, la querella
en que perdí la causa de mi huella.

Luego, haciendo del átomo una espiga,
encenderé mis hoces al pie de ella
y la espiga será por fin espiga.

and almost, in proportion, almost heighten myself.
For: to know why life is this dog,
why I weep, why
puckered, oafish and unreliable I was born
screaming;
to know, to understand this
in terms of a competent alphabet,
would be to suffer for an ingrate.

And no! No! No! Still less tricks or trappings!
Grief, yes, with a yes firm and frantic,
leathery, rapacious, will and won't, bird and sky;
grief, yes, with the whole of one's fly.
A match between two sobs, theft of a single bliss,
unpained via on which I endure in galoshes
the velocity of walking blind.

Wedding march

At the head of my own acts
crown in hand, battalion of gods,
the negative sign at my neck, enormous
the match and the rush, struck stupid
of soul and courage, by two blows

straight to my gaze; throwing it back;
the boundaries, dynamic, fierce;
swallowing down my loose tears,

I'll fire myself, my itch will burn
my key will burn, the choked yearning
where I lost the cause of my track.

Then making the atom into an ear
I'll burn my sickles near her
and the ear will at last be ear.

El alma qué sufrió de ser su cuerpo

Tú sufres de una glándula endocrínica, se ve,
o, quizá,
sufres de mí, de mi sagacidad escueta, tácita.
Tú padeces del diáfano antropoide, allá, cerca,
donde está la tiniebla tenebrosa.
Tú das vuelta al sol, agarrándote el alma,
extendiendo tus juanes corporales
y ajustándote el cuello; eso se ve.
Tú sabes lo que te duele,
lo que te salta al anca,
lo que baja por ti con soga al suelo.
Tú, pobre hombre, vives; no lo niegues,
si mueres; no lo niegues,
si mueres de tu edad ¡ay! y de tu época.
Y, aunque llores, bebes,
y, aunque sangres, alimentas a tu híbrido colmillo,
a tu vela tristona y a tus partes.
Tú sufres, tú padeces y tú vuelves a sufrir horriblemente,
desgraciado mono,
jovencito de Darwin,
alguacil que me atisbas, atrocísimo microbio.

Y tú lo sabes a tal punto,
que lo ignoras, soltándote a llorar.
Tú, luego, has nacido; eso
también se ve de lejos, infeliz y cállate,
y soportas la calle que te dio la suerte
y a tu hombligo interrogas: ¿dónde? ¿cómo?

Amigo mío, estás completamente,
hasta el pelo, en el año treinta y ocho,
nicolás o santiago, tal o cual,
estés contigo o con tu aborto o con-
migo,
y cautivo en tu enorme libertad,

The soul that suffered from being its body

Obviously, you're suffering from a hormonal gland,
or maybe
you're suffering from me, from my stark, tacit sagacity.
You are the victim of this anthropoidal diaphane, right here
where the tenebrous tenebrae are.
You turn around the sun, grabbing your soul,
stretching your corporal members
and adjusting your neck; can't you see it.
You know what's hurting you,
what's jumping on your rump,
what descends through you by rope to the floor.
You live, poor man; don't deny it,
if you, die; don't deny it,
if you die of your age, ay! and of your epoch.
And even if you weep, you drink,
and even if you bleed, you feed your hybrid canine,
your wistful flame and your nether parts.
You suffer, you're hurt and once more you suffer horribly,
unfortunate ape,
Darwin's laddie,
bailiff spying me out, atrocious microbe.

And you so much know it
that you don't know it, bursting forth to cry.
Therefore you have been born; that
also is clear from way off, fool so be quiet,
and you tolerate the street which gave you your chance
but you question your umbilicus: where? how?

My friend, you are completely
up to your hair, in year thirty-eight,
nicholas or james, what does it matter,
just Be to yourself or to your abortionem or to
me,
and captive in your enormous freedom,

arrastrado por tu hércules autónomo . . .
Pero si tú calulas en tus dedos hasta dos,
es peor; no lo niegues, hermanito.

¿Que no? ¿Que sí, pero que no?
¡Pobre mono! . . . ¡Dame la pata! . . . No. La mano, he dicho.
¡Salud! ¡Y sufre!

Telúrica y magnética

  ¡Mecánica sincera y peruanísma
la del cerro colorado!
¡Suelo teórico y práctico!
¡Surcos inteligentes; ejemplo: el monolito y su cortejo!
¡Papales, cebadales, alfalfares, cosa buena!
¡Cultivos que integra una asombrosa jerarquía de útiles
y que integran con viento los mujidos,
las aguas con su sorda antigüedad!

  ¡Cuarternarios maíces, de opuestos natalicos,
los oigo por los pies cómo se alejan,
los huelo retornar cuando la tierra
tropieza con la técnica del cielo.
¡Molécula exabrupto! ¡Átomo terso!

  ¡Oh campos humanos!
¡Solar y nutricia ausencia de la mar,
y sentimiento oceánico de todo!
¡Oh climas encontrados dentro del oro, listos!
¡Oh campo intelectual de cordillera,
con religión, con campo, con patitos!
¡Paquidermos en prosa cuando pasan
y en verso cuando páranse!
¡Roedores que miran con sentimiento judicial en torno!
¡Oh patrióticos asnos de mi vida!

dragged along by your autonomous hercules ...
But if you count on two fingers,
it's worse; don't deny it, little brother.
It's not? It is, but it isn't?
Poor ape! ... Give me your foot! Your hand I mean.
Good luck! And bear up!

Bedrock and Lode

Straight mechanics and most Peruvian
that red ridge!
Theoretical and practical ground!
Intelligent furrows; example: the monolith and its circle!
Crops of potatoes, barley, alfalfa, good things!
Food adapted to an astounding heirarchy of utensils
and which integrates bellowing with wind,
the waters with their mute antiquity!

Quaternary maize plants, of hybrid birth,
through my feet I hear them moving away.
I smell them return when the earth
runs across the technical sky.
Impetuous molecule! Terse atom!

Oh human fields!
Solar and nourishing absence of sea,
and oceanic sentiment in everything!
Oh climes found within gold, alert!
Oh intellectual field of the cordillera,
with religion, with countryside, with ducklings!
Pachiderms of prose as they pass
and of poetry when they come to a stop!
Rodents who look on in their sceptical circumspection!
Oh patriotic jackasses of my life!

¡Vicuña, descendiente
nacional y graciosa de mi mono!
¡Oh luz que dista apenas un espejo de la sombra,
que es vida con el punto y, con la línea, polvo
y que por eso acato, subiendo por la idea de mi osamenta!

      ¡Siega en época del dilatado molle,
del farol que colgaron de la sien
y del que descolgaron de la barreta espléndida!
¡Ángeles de corral,
aves por un descuido de la cresta!
¡Cuya o cuy para comerlos fritos
con el bravo rocoto de los templos!
(¿Cóndores? ¡Me friegan los cóndores!)
¡Leños cristianos en gracia
al tronco feliz y al tallo competente!
¡Familia de los líquenes,
especies en formación basáltica que yo
respeto
desde este modestísimo papel!
¡Cuatro operaciones, os sustriago
para salvar al roble y hundirlo en bueno ley!
¡Cuestas en infraganti!
¡Auquénidos llorosos, almas mias!
¡Sierra de mi Perú, Perú del mundo,
y Perú al pie del orbe; yo me adhiero!
¡Estrellas matutinas si os aromo
quemando hojas de coca en este cráneo,
y cenitales, si destapo,
de un solo sombrerazo, mis diez templos!
¡Brazo de siembra, bájate, y a pie!
¡Lluvia a base del mediodía,
bajo al techo de tejas donde muerde
la infatigable altura
y la tórtola corta en tres su trino!
¡Rotación de tardes modernas
y finas madrugadas arqueológicas!

Vicuña, national
and silly descendent of my monkey!
Oh light a mirror-width from shade,
which is life with the point and, with the line, dust
and this I respect, rising through the idea of my skeleton!

Harvest in the epoch of the swollen molle tree,
when they hung the lantern from their brow
and took down the splendid pick!
Farmyard angels,
birds from a careless crest!
Guinea pigs toasted for eating
with the fierce chile of the temples!
(Condors? I've had it with condors!)
Christian forests by virtue
of the fortunate trunk and reliable stem!

Families of lichen,
species in basalt formation that I
respect
from this most modest paper!
Four operations, I deduct you
to spare the oak and sink it in high assay!
Hills in fragranti!
Weeping camelids, my souls!
Sierra of my Peru, Peru of the world,
and Peru at the foot of the globe; I'll stick with you!
Stars of the morning, when I perfume you
with burning coca leaves in this skull,
of the zeniths, if I could uncover,
in one sweep of the hat, my ten temples!
Sowing arm, get down, and on foot!

Rain, always at noontide,
under the tiled roof where
the relentless altitude bites
and the dove cuts its trill in three!

¡Indio después del hombre y antes de él!
¡Lo entiendo todo en dos flautas
y me doy a entender en una quena!
¡Y los demás, me las pelan!…

ESPAÑA, APARTA DE MÍ ESTE CÁLIZ

I: Himno a los voluntarios de la República

Voluntario de España, miliciano
de huesos fidedignos, cuando marcha a morir tu corazón,
cuando marcha a matar con su agonía
mundial, no sé verdaderamente
qué hacer, dónde ponerme; corro, escribo, aplaudo,
lloro, atisbo, destrozo, apagan, digo
a mi pecho que acabe, al bien, que venga,
y quiero desgraciarme:
descúbrome la frente impersonal hasta tocar
el vaso de la sangre, me detengo,
detienen mi tamaño esas famosas caídas de arquitecto
con las que se honra el animal que me honra;
refluyen mis instintos a sus sogas,
humea ante mi tumba la alegría
y, otra vez, sin saber qué hacer, sin nada, déjame,
desde mi piedra en blanco, déjame
solo,
cuadrumano, más acá, mucho más lejos,
al no caber entre mis manos tu largo rato extático,
quiebro contra tu rapidez de doble filo
mi pequeñez en traje de grandeza!

Un día diurno, claro, atento, fértil

Rotation of modern afternoons
and fine archeological dawnings!
Indian after man and before him!
I understand it all on two flutes
and make myself understood on a quena!
For the rest, let them have it!...

SPAIN, TAKE AWAY THIS CUP FROM ME

I: Hymn to the volunteers of the Republic

Volunteer of Spain, militiaman
of sound bones, when your heart marches to die,
when it marches to kill with its world-
agony, I really don't know
what to do, where to put myself; I run, write, applaud,
weep, spy, destroy, they put it out, I say to
my chest it should end, to good it should come;
and I want to ruin myself;
I bare my impersonal brow so much I touch
my blood's vessel, I catch myself,
my size is caught in those famous architect's lapses
with which the animal that honours me honours itself;
my instincts surge back into their ropes,
gaiety steams before my tomb
and, once again, not knowing what to do, devoid, leave me,
from my unwritten stone, leave me,
alone,
quadrumane, nearer home, way beyond,
I find your long ecstatic while doesn't fit between my hands,
and against your double-edged rapidity
I dash my smallness in its grand clothing!

One diurnal day, clear, attentive, fertile

¡oh bienio, el de los lóbregos semestres suplicantes,
por el que iba la pólvora mordiéndose los codos!
¡oh dura pena y más duros pedernales!
¡oh frenos los tascados por el pueblo!
Un día prendió el pueblo su fósforo cautivo, oró de cólera
y soberanamente pleno, circular,
cerró su natalicio con manos electivas;
arrastraban candado ya los déspotas
y en el candado, sus bacterias muertas ...

¿Batallas? ¡No! ¡Pasiones! Y pasiones precedidas
de dolores con rejas de esperanzas,
¡de dolores de pueblo con esperanzas de hombres!
¡Muerte y pasión de paz, las populares!
¡Muerte y pasión guerreras entre olivos, entendámosnos!
Tal en tu aliento cambian de agujas atmosféricas los vientos
y de llave las tumbas en tu pecho,
tu frontal elevándose a primera potencia de martirio.

El mundo exclama: "¡Cosas de españoles!" Y es
          verdad. Consideremos,
durante una balanza, a quema ropa,
a Calderón, dormido sobre la cola de un anfibio muerto,
o a Cervantes, diciendo: "Mi reino es de este mundo, pero
también del otro": ¡punta y filo en dos papeles!
Contemplemos a Goya, de hinojos y rezando ante un espejo,
a Coll, el paladín en cuyo asalto cartesiano
tuvo un sudor de nube el paso llano,
o a Quevedo, ese abuelo instantáneo de los dinamiteros,
o a Cajal, devorado por su pequeño infinito, o todavía
a Teresa, mujer, que muere porque no muere,
o a Lina Odena, en pugna en más de un punto con Teresa ...
(Todo acto o voz genial viene del pueblo
y va hacia él, de frente o transmitido
por incesantes briznas, por el humo rosado
de amargas contraseñas sin fortuna.)
Así tu criatura, miliciano, así tu exangüe criatura,

(oh biennium of murky supplicant semesters,
through which gunpowder went biting its elbows!
Oh hard pain and harder flints!
Oh bits champed at by the people!)
One day the people lit their captive match, prayed with rage
and sovereignly full, circular,
made their birthright fast with elective hands;
the despots were trailing padlocks by now
and in the padlock, their dead bacteria . . .

Battles? No! Passions! And passions preceded
by aches barred with hopes,
by aches of the people with men's hopes! ·
Death and passion for peace, the popular ones!
Martial death and passion among olive trees, let's be plain!
So, in your breath, the winds change their atmospheric needles
and the tombs in your chest change keys,
with your forehead raising itself to the first power of martyrdom.

The world exclaims: "A Spanish affair" And it's true.
        Let's consider,
point-blank,
Calderon, asleep on the tail of a dead amphibian,
or Cervantes, saying: "My kingdom is of this world, but
also of the next": point and edge in two roles!
Let's look at Goya, kneeling and praying before a mirror,
at Coll, the paladin in whose Cartesian assault
solid steps had the sweat of a cloud,
or at Quevedo, that instant godfather of dynamiters,
or at Cajal, devoured by this tiny infinity, or yet
at Teresa, a woman, who dies because she does not die,
or at Lina Odena, at odds with Teresa on more than one count . . .
(Every genial act or voice comes from the people
or goes towards them, directly or transmitted
through repeated slivers, through the pink smoke
or bitter no-good passwords.)
Thus your child, miliciano, thus your anemic child,

agitada por una piedra inmóvil,
se sacrifica, apártase,
decae para arriba y por su llama incombustible sube,
sube hasta los débiles,
distribuyendo españas a los toros,
toros a las palomas ...
Proletario que mueres de universo, ¡ en qué frenética armonía
acabará tu grandeza, tu miseria, tu vorágine impelente,
tu violencia metódica, tu caos teórico y práctico, tu gana
dantesca, españolísima, de amar, aunque sea a traición, a tu enemigo!
¡Liberador ceñido de grilletes,
sin cuyo esfuerzo hasta hoy continuaría sin asas la extensión,
vagarían acéfalos los clavos,
antiguo, lento, colorado, el día,
nuestros amados cascos, insepultos!
¡Campesino caído con tu verde follaje por el hombre,
con la inflexión social de tu meñique,
con tu buey que se queda, con tu física,
también con tu palabra atada a un palo
y tu cielo arrendado
y con la arcilla inserta en tu cansancio
y la que estaba en tu uña, caminando!
¡Constructores
agrícolas, civiles y guerreros,
de la activa, hormigueante eternidad: estaba escrito
que vosotros haríais la luz, entornando
con la muerte vuestros ojos;
que, a la caída cruel de vuestras bocas,
vendrá en siete bandejas la abundancia, todo
en el mundo será de oro súbito
y el oro,
fabulosos mendigos de vuestra propia secreción de sangre,
y el oro mismo será entonces de oro!

¡Se amarán todos los hombres
y comerán tomados de las puntas de vuestros pañuelos tristes
y beberán en nombre

stirred by a motionless stone,
grows in sacrifice and distance,
drops upwards and rises along her incombustible flame,
rises up to the weak,
distributing spains to the bulls,
bulls to the doves ...
Proletarian, you who die of universe, in what frantic harmony
your greatness will end, your lack, your driving tornado,
your methodic violence, your theoretical and practical chaos, your
Dantesque and most Spanish desire to love your enemy to betrayal!
Fettered liberator,
without your effort space would still today be handleless,
nails would wander acephalous,
the day ancient, slow, and red,
and our loved skulls, unburied!
Peasant who fell for man with your green,
with the social inflexion of your little finger,
with your ox that remains, with your physics,
also with your word tied to a stick
and your rented sky
and clay crammed in your tiredness
and the clay under your nail, walking!
Builders,
agricultural, civil and martial,
of a busy, teeming eternity: it was written
that you would create light rolling back
your eyes in death;
that, with the cruel demise of your mouths,
abundance will come on seven salvers, everything
in the world will be sudden gold
and the gold,
you fabulous supplicants of your own secreted blood,
and gold itself will then be gold!

All men will love each other
and will eat holding the corners of your sad handkerchieves
and will drink in the name

de vuestras gargantas infaustas!
Descansarán andando al pie de esta carrera,
sollozarán pensando en vuestras órbitas, venturosos
serán y al son
de vuestro atroz retorno, florecido, innato,
ajustarán mañana sus quehaceres, sus figuras soñadas y cantadas!

¡Unos mismos zapatos irán bien al que asciende
sin vías a su cuerpo
y al que baja hasta la forma de su alma!
¡Entrelazándose hablarán los mudos, los tullidos andarán!
¡Verán, ya de regreso, los ciegos
y palpitando escucharán los sordos!
¡Sabrán los ignorantes, ignorarán los sabios!
¡Serán dados los besos que no pudisteis dar!
¡Sólo la muerte morirá! ¡La hormiga
traerá pedacitos de pan al elefante encadenado
a su brutal delicadeza; volverán
los niños abortados a nacer perfectos, espaciales
y trabajarán todos los hombres,
engendrarán todos los hombres,
comprenderán todos los hombres!

¡Obrero, salvador, redentor nuestro,
perdónanos, hermano, nuestras deudas!
Como dice un tambor al redoblar, en sus adagios:
¡qué jamás tan efímero, tu espalda!
¡qué siempre tan cambiante, tu perfil!

¡Voluntario italiano, entre cuyos animales de batalla
un león abisinio va cojeando!
¡Voluntario soviético, marchando a la cabeza de tu pecho universal!
¡Voluntarios del sur, del norte, del oriente
y tú, el occidental, cerrando el canto fúnebre del alba!
¡Soldado conocido, cuyo nombre
desfila en el sonido de un abrazo!
¡Combatiente que la tierra criara, armándote

of your unlucky throats!
They'll relax walking close to this course,
they'll sob thinking of your orbits, fortunate
they'll be and at the sound
of your awful return, an unborn flower,
they'll adjust their tasks tomorrow, their dreamed and sung figures!

The same shoes will suit the man ascending
tractless to his body
and the man going right down to his soul's form!
The dumb will speak intertwined, the maimed will walk!
The blind, returning now, will see
and, quivering, the deaf will hear!
The ignorant will be wise, the wise ignorant!
The kisses you could not give will be given!
Only death will die! The ant
will bring crumbs of bread to the elephant enchained
in its brutal delicacy; aborted children
will be born again perfect, spatial
and all men will work,
all men will engender,
all men will understand!

Worker, our saviour and redeemer,
forgive us, brother, our trespasses!
As the drum says when it sounds, in its adagios:
how ephemeral a never, your back!
how Protean an ever, your profile!

Italian volunteer, among whose animals of battle
an Abyssinian lion goes limping!
Soviet volunteer, marching at the head of your universal heart!
Volunteers from the south, from the north, from the east
and you, the western one, closing the funeral chant of the dawn!
Known soldier, whose name
files past in the sound of an embrace!
Combatant whom the earth created, armed

de polvo,
calzándote de imanes positivos,
vigentes tus creencias personales,
distinto de carácter, íntima tu férula,
el cutis inmediato,
andándote tu idioma por los hombros
y el alma coronada de guijarros!
¡Voluntario fajado de tu zona fría,
templada o tórrida,
héroes a la redonda,
víctima en columna de vencedores:
en España, en Madrid, están llamando
a matar, voluntarios de la vida!

Porque en España matan, otros matan
al niño, a su juguete que se para,
a la madre Rosenda esplendorosa,
al viejo Adán que hablaba en alta voz con su caballo
y al perro que dormía en la escalera.
¡Matan al libro, tiran a sus verbos auxiliares.
a su indefensa página primera!
Matan el caso exacto de la estatua,
al sabio, a su bastón, a su colega,
al barbero de al lado—me cortó posiblemente,
pero buen hombre y, luego, infortunado;
al mendigo que ayer cantaba enfrente,
a la enfermera que hoy pasó llorando,
al sacerdote a cuestas con la altura tenaz de sus rodillas ...

¡Voluntarios,
por la vida, por los buenos, matad
a la muerte, matad a los malos!
¡Hacedlo por la libertad de todos,
del explotado y del explotador,
por la paz indolora—la sospecho
cuando duermo al pie de mi frente
y más cuando circulo dando voces—

with dust,
shod with positive magnets,
your personal beliefs in force,
your character distinct, your rod intimate,
your skin immediate,
your language wreathing your shoulders
and your soul crowned with pebbles!
Volunteer sashed with your cold zone,
temperate or torrid zone,
heroes round,
victim in a column of conquerors;
in Spain, in Madrid, they're calling
you to kill, volunteers of life!

For in Spain they kill, others kill
the boy, his toy which comes to a stop,
resplendent mother Rosenda,
old Adam who talked aloud with his horse
and the dog which slept on the stairs.
They kill the book, shoot at its auxiliary verbs,
at its defenceless first page!
They kill the exact case of the statue,
the scholar, his stick, his colleague,
the barber next door—he may have cut me,
but was a good man and, then, unfortunate;
the beggar yesterday who sang opposite,
the nurse who went by crying today,
the priest staggering under the persistent height of his knees ...

Volunteers:
for life, for good men, kill
death, kill the evil men!
Do it for the freedom of all,
of the exploited and the exploiter,
for painless peace—I intuit it
when I sleep right by my brow
and more when I go round shouting out—

y hacedlo, voy diciendo,
por el analfabeto a quien escribo,
por el genio descalzo y su cordero,
por los camaradas caídos,
sus cenizas abrazadas al cadáver de un camino!

Para que vosotros,
voluntarios de España y del mundo, vinierais,
soñé que era yo bueno, y era para ver
vuestra sangre, voluntarios ...
De esto hace mucho pecho, muchas ansias,
muchos camellos en edad de orar.
Marcha hoy de vuestra parte el bien ardiendo,
os siguen con cariño los reptiles de pestaña inmanente
y, a dos pasos, a uno,
la dirección del agua que corre a ver su límite antes que arda.

IV: Los mendigos ...

Los mendigos pelean por España,
mendigando en París, en Roma, en Praga
y refrendando así, con mano gótica, rogante,
los pies de los Apóstoles, en Londres, en New York, en Méjico.
Los pordioseros luchan suplicando infernalmente
a Dios por Santander,
la lid en que ya nadie es derrotado.
Al sufrimiento antiguo
danse, encarnízanse en llorar plomo social
al pie del individuo,
y atacan a gemidos los mendigos,
matando con tan sólo ser mendigos.

Ruegos de infantería,
en que el arma ruega del metal para arriba,
y ruega la ira, más acá de la pólvora iracunda.

and do it, I keep saying,
for the illiterate man to whom I write,
for the barefoot genius and his lamb,
for fallen comrades,
their ashes embracing the corpse of a road!

So that you,
volunteers of Spain and the world, would come,
I dreamt I was good, and worthy of seeing
your blood, volunteers ...
Of this comes much heart, many worries,
many camels of an age to pray.
Today good marches in flames on your behalf,
reptiles with immanent eyelashes follow you with affection
and, two steps, one step behind,
the direction of the water coursing to see its limit before it burns.

IV: The beggars ...

The beggars fight for Spain,
begging in Paris, in Rome, in Prague
and so authenticate, with beseeching Gothic hands,
the Apostles' feet, in London, in New York, in Mexico.
They enlist pleading hellishly
to God for Santander,
the contest no-one lost by now.
To ancient suffering
they give themselves, they snarl weeping social lead
at the individual,
and attack by groans,
kill just by being beggars.

An infantryman's plea
in which the weapon pleads upwards from the metal,
and wrath pleads, nearer home than the angry powder.

Tácitos escuadrones que disparan,
con cadencia mortal, su mansedumbre,
desde un umbral, desde sí mismos, ¡ay! desde sí mismos.
Potenciales guerreros
sin calcetines al calzar el trueno,
satánicos, numéricos,
arrastrando sus títulos de fuerza,
migaja al cinto,
fusil doble calibre: sangre y sangre.
¡El poeta saluda al sufrimiento armado!

IX: Pequeño responso a un héroe de la República

Un libro quedó al borde de su cintura muerta,
un libro retoñaba de su cadáver muerto.
Se llevaron al héroe,
y corpórea y aciaga entró su boca en nuestro aliento;
sudamos todos, el ombligo a cuestas;
caminantes las lunas nos seguían;
también sudaba de tristeza el muerto.

Y un libro, en la batalla de Toledo,
un libro, artás un libro, arriba un libro, retoñaba del cadáver.

Poesía del pómulo morado, entre el decirlo
y el callarlo.
poesía en la carta moral que acompañara
a su corazón.
Quedóse el libro y nada más, que no hay
insectos en la tumba,
y quedó al borde de su manga el aire remojándose
y haciéndose gaseoso, infinito.

Todos sudamos, el ombligo a cuestas,
también sudaba de tristeza el muerto

Tacit squadrons who fire
their meekness with mortal cadence
from a doorway, from themselves, alas! from themselves.
Potential warriors
shoeing their bare soles with thunder,
satanic, numerical,
dragging along their regular names,
breadcrumb at the hip,
a double-barrelled rifle: blood and blood.
The poet salutes armed suffering!

IX: Small liturgy for a hero of the Republic

A book remained at the margin of his dead waist,
a book was sprouting from his dead corpse.
They carried the hero away,
and corporeal and ominous his mouth entered our breath;
we all sweated under the load of our navels;
the moons travelled after us;
the dead man was also sweating with sadness.

And a book, at the battle of Toledo,
a book, a book behind, a book above, was sprouting from the corpse.

Poetry of the morat cheek, between saying it
and keeping it quiet,
poetry in the moral message that had accompanied
his heart.
The book remained and nothing else, for there are
no insects in the grave,
and the air remained at the margin of his sleeve steeping itself
and becoming gaseous, infinite.

We all sweated under the load of our navels,
the dead man was also sweating with sadness

y un libro, yo lo vi sentidamente,
un libro, atrás un libro, arriba un libro
retoñó del cadáver exabrupto.

XII: Masa

Al fin de la batalla,
y muerto el combatiente, vino hacia él un hombre
y le dijo: "¡No mueras; te amo tanto!"
Pero el cadáver ¡ay! siguió muriendo.

Se le acercaron dos y repitiéronle:
"¡No nos dejes! ¡Valor! ¡Vuelve a la vida!"
Pero el cadáver ¡ay! siguió muriendo.

Acudieron a él veinte, cien, mil, quinientos mil,
clamando : "¡Tanto amor, y no poder nada contra la muerte!"
Pero el cadáver ¡ay! siguió muriendo.

Le rodearon millones de individuos,
con un ruego común: "¡Quédate, hermano!"
Pero el cadáver ¡ay! siguió muriendo.

Entonces, todos los hombres de la tierra
le rodearon; les vio el cadáver triste, emocionado;
incorporóse lentamente,
abrazó al primer hombre; echóse a andar . . .

and a book, I saw it feelingly,
a book, a book behind, a book above
abrupt bud of the corpse.

XII: Mass

At the end of the battle,
with the combatant dead, a man came up
and told him: "Don't die, I love you so much!"
But the corpse, alas! went on dying.

Two others came up and said to him again:
"Don't leave us! Courage! Come back to life!"
But the corpse, alas! went on dying.

Twenty, a hundred, a thousand, five hundred thousand ran up to him,
crying out: "So much love and no way of countering death!"
But the corpse, alas! went on dying.

Millions of individuals stood round him,
with a common plea : "Stay here brother!"
But the corpse, alas! went on dying.

Then all the men on earth
stood round him; the sad corpse saw them, with emotion;
he got up slowly,
embraced the first man; began to walk ...

XV: España, aparta de mí este cáliz

Niños del mundo,
si cae España—digo, es un decir—
si cae
del cielo abajo su antebrazo que asen,
en cabestro, dos láminas terrestres;
niños, ¡qué edad la de las sienes cóncavas!
¡qué temprano en el sol lo que os decía!
¡qué pronto en vuestro pecho el ruido anciano!
¡qué viejo vuestro 2 en el cuaderno!

Niños del mundo, está
la madre España con su vientre a cuestas;
está nuestra maestra con sus férulas,
está madre y maestra,
cruz y madera, porque os dio la altura,
vértigo y división y suma, niños;
está con ella, padres procesales!

Si cae—digo, es un decir—si cae
España, de la tierra para abajo,
niños, ¡cómo vais a cesar de crecer!
¡cómo va a castigar el año al mes!
¡cómo van a quedarse en diez los dientes,
en palote el diptongo, la medalla en llanto!
¡Cómo va el corderillo a continuar
atado por la pata al gran tintero!
¡Cómo vais a bajar las gradas del alfabeto
hasta la letra en que nació la pena!

Niños,
hijos de los guerreros, entretanto,
bajad la voz, que España está ahora mismo repartiendo
la energía entre el reino animal,
las florecillas, los cometas y los hombres.
¡Bajad la voz, que está

XV: Spain, take away this cup from me

Children of the world,
if Spain falls—just supposing—
if down from the sky
her forearm falls, let two
terrestrial sheets catch it in a sling;
children: what age in those concave temples!
how early in the sun my message to you!
how prompt in your chest the ancient noise!
how old your 2 in the exercise book!

Children of the world, Spain the mother
has her belly as a load;
she stands as our teacher with her canes,
as mother and teacher,
cross and wood, because she gave you height,
vertigo and division and addition, children;
it's her matter, quibbling parents!

If she falls—just supposing—if Spain
falls down from the earth,
how you'll stop growing, children!
how the year will chastise its months!
how teeth will bunch into ten,
diphthongs into pen strokes, into weeping the medal!
How the little lamb will stay
bound by its leg to the great inkwell!
How you'll descend the alphabet steps
to the letter in which pain was born!

Children,
fighters' sons, lower
your voices the while, for this very moment Spain is sharing out
energy among the animal kingdom,
the little flowers, the comets and men,
Lower your voices, for she's deep

cou su rigor, que es grande, sin saber
qué hacer, y está en su mano
la calavera hablando y habla y habla,
la calavera, aquélla de la trenza,
la calavera, aquélla de la vida!

¡Bajad la voz, os digo;
bajad la voz, el canto de las sílabas, el llanto
de la materia y el rumor menor de las pirámides, y aun
el de las sienes que andan con dos piedras!
¡Bajad el aliento, y si
el antebrazo baja,
si las férulas suenan, si es la noche,
si el cielo cabe en dos limbos terrestres,
si hay ruido en el sonido de las puertas,
si tardo,
si no veis a nadie, si os asustan
los lápices sin punta, si la madre
España cae—digo, es un decir—
salid, niños del mundo; id a buscarla! ...

into her intensity, for she's great and doesn't know
what to do, and in her hand is
the skull speaking and it speaks and speaks,
the skull, the one with the braid,
the skull, the one of life!

Lower your voices, I tell you;
quieten your voices, the syllables' song, the weeping
of matter and the lesser murmur of pyramids, and even
the murmur of your temples under the weight of two stones!
Lower your breath, and if
her forearm comes down,
if her canes swish, if it's night,
if the sky fits into two terrestial limbos,
if there's noise in the sound of doors,
if I arrive late,
if you don't see anyone, if blunt pencils
scare you, if Spain
the mother falls—just supposing—
go out children of the world, go and find her ...

PATRICIA GALVAO

ALBUM DE PAGU, 1929

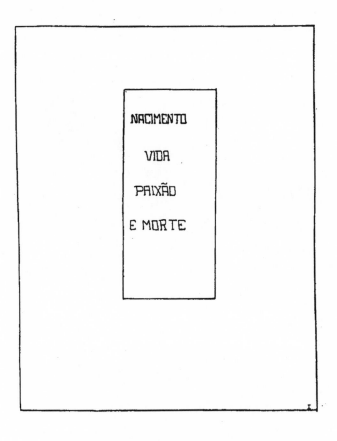

Birth
Life
Passion
& Death

Beyond, much beyond the pink Martinelli skyscraper ...
... which Martinelly-wise opens its 154 throats ...
    She was a daughter of the moon ...
    She was a daughter of the sun ...
Of the moon, who appears serene & soft in the sky, forever suckling
black St. George's knight ... paunchy ...
Of the father sun, noble and beloved feature of futurist paintings,
Her father enjoys a bit of fondling
& Pagú was born ...

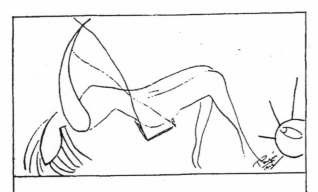

The insensitive rectangle of Cabreúva town collects
the volcanic delight of my vitality ...
I want to go very high ... very high ...
feeling delicious superiority
you see on the other side of the wall there's
something I want to peep at.

natureza diabolica
calor infernal
cores sadias
taboas. musgos. lodo.
soltava papagaios e voltava pra casa sem baton.

devilish nature
hellish heat
healthy hues
bull rushes, moss, mud.
She would fly kites & come home without lipstick

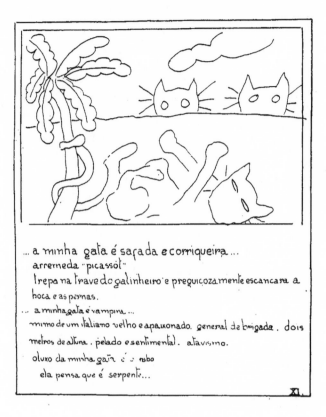

... my cat is kinky and trivial
she imitates "picassol"
climbs on the hen coup perch & lazily opens her
mouth & her legs.
... my cat is a vampire ...
the darling of an old & passionate Italian. brigadier general. two
meters tall. bald & sentimental. atavism.
my cat's forte is her tail
she thinks it's a snake ...

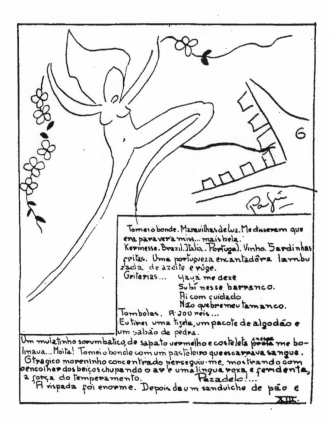

I took the tram. Wonders of light. They told me it was
to see the most beauteous ... queen.
A fest. Brazil. Italy. Portugal. Wine. Fried
sardines. A lovely Portuguese woman
covered with oil & rouge.
People shouting ...   Missy please let me
                        mount this log.
                        Lordie go easy
                        you're cracking my clog.
Tombolas. 200 reis a go ...
My prize was a bowl, cottonwool & a bar of soap.

A sad mulatto with red shoes & frizzy sideburns
fondled me ... Doggo! I took the tram with a dumpling man who
    spat blood.
The tragic & intense darkie followed me, showing the measure of
his temper with the chops that sucked in the air & a purple
sore-ridden tongue.   Nightmare!
The spark was enormous. After a sausage
sandwich I slept, embracing the broom handle, a kitchen knife under
my pillow ... Doggo! I dreamt of the sad
mulatto with the sore-ridden tongue ...

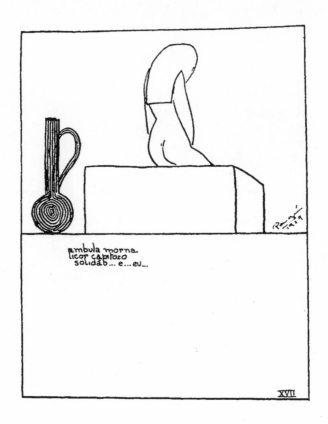

tepid vase
choice liqueur
solitude ... and ... me

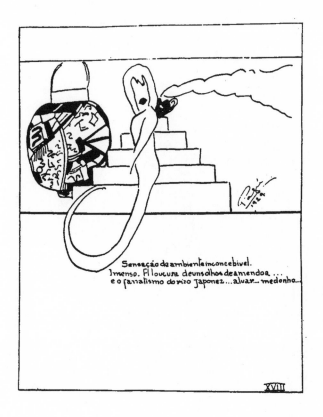

An inconceivable sense of environment.
Immense. Crazy almond eyes ...
and fanatical Japanese laughter ... all white ... dreadful ...

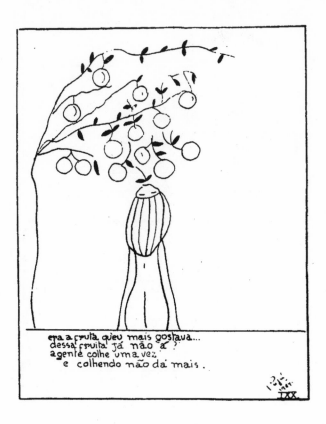

It was the fruit I liked the most ...
it's no longer around
we pick it once
once picked it's gone.

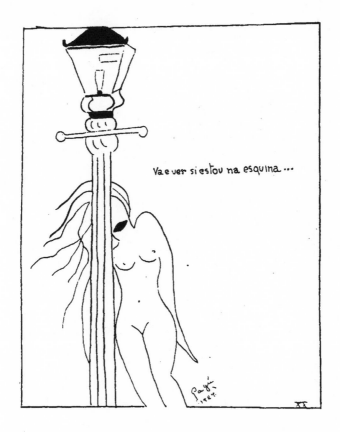

Go see if I'm at the corner

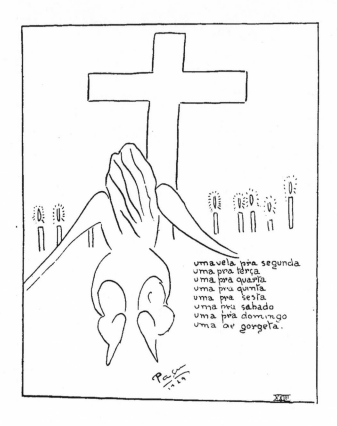

one candle for Monday
one for Tuesday
one for Wednesday
one for Thursday
one for Friday
one for Saturday
one for Sunday
one as a tip

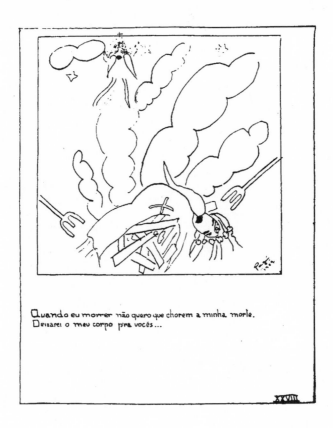

When I die don't weep over my death.
I'll leave my body for you ...

LAST POEMS (1960-62)

Canal

Nada mais sou que um canal
Seria verde se fosse o caso
Mas estão mortas todas as esperanças
Sou um canal
Sabem vocês o que é ser um canal?
Apenas um canal?

Evidentemente um canal tem as suas nervuras
As suas nebulosidades
As suas algas
Nereidazinhas verdes, às vezes amarelas
Mas por favor
Não pensem que estou pretendendo falar
Em bandeiras
Isso não

Gosto de bandeiras alastradas ao vento
Bandeiras de navio
As ruas são as mesmas.
O asfalto com os mesmos buracos,
Os inferninhos acesos,
O que está acontecendo?
É verdade que está ventando noroeste,
Há garotos nos bares
Há, não sei mais o que há.
Digamos que seja a lua nova
Que seja esta plantinha voacejando na minha frente.
Lembranças dos meus amigos que morreram
Lembranças de todas as coisas ocorridas
Há coisas no ar . . .
Digamos que seja a lua nova
Iluminando o canal
Seria verde se fosse o caso
Mas estão mortas todas as esperanças
Sou um canal.

Canal

I am nothing—a canal
I would be green if that were the case
But all those hopes are dead
I am a canal
Do you know what it's like
To be a canal, merely a canal?

Evidently a canal has her nerve lines
Her nebulous mists
And her algas under the sun
micro nereids, green and yellow nymphs
But if you please
Let's not talk about flags
or expeditions to the interior
No, none of that

I like banners spinning on the wind
The flags of ships
The same street scenes.
Asphalt with the same old holes,
Nightclubs enkindled in hell,
What's going on in there?
It's true, the Nor'wester is hot,
There are punks in the bars
And who knows what else.
Let's say there's a new moon
This greenery waving up ahead.
Memories of friends who died
Remembrances of all that happened
There are things on the air . . .
Maybe a new moon
Lighting up the canal
I would be green if such were the case
But all those hopes are dead
I am a canal.

Um peixe

Um pedaço de trapo que fosse
Atirado numa estrada
Em que todos pisam
Um pouco de brisa
Uma gota de chuva
Uma lágrima
Um pedaço de livro
Uma letra ou um número
Um nada, pelo menos
Desesperadamente nada.

Fósforos de segurança

Fósforos de segurança
Indústrias tais
Fatais.
Isso veio hoje numa pequena caixa
Que achei demasiado cretina
Porque além de toda essa história
De São Paulo—Brasil
Dava indicações do nome da fábrica.
Que eu não vou dizer
Porque afinal o meu mister não é dizer
Nome de indústria
Que não gosto nem um pouquinho
De publicidade
A não ser que
Isso tudo venha com um nome de família
Instituição abalizada
Que atrapalha a vida de quem nada quer saber
Com ela.
Ela, ela, ela.

A Fish

An old rag, scrap of cloth
Tossed on the street
Trod upon by one and all
A slight gust
A streak of rain
A tear drop
A torn page of some book
A letter or a number
A nothing—nothing less
Hopelessly nothing.

Safety Matches

Industrial stuff like that—
Fatal.
This arrived today on a little box
Which was just too cretinous
Because, besides the gossipy history
About São Paulo—Brazil
It carried the imprimatur of the factory.
Which I'll not repeat
Since it's not my duty to give you
The name of an industry
Nor do I like, even a little bit,
Publicity
Unless it comes with a family name—
Vaunted trust
Which ensnares the lives of those
Who want no part
Of it.
It. It. It.

Nothing

Nada nada nada
Nada mais do que nada
Porque vocês querem que exista apenas o nada
Pois existe o só nada
Um párabrisa partido uma perna quebrada
O nada
Fisionomias massacradas
Tipóias em meus amigos
Portas arrombadas
Abertas para o nada
Um choro de criança
Uma lágrima de mulher à-toa
Que quer dizer nada
Um quarto meio escuro
Com um abajur quebrado
Meninas que dançavam
Que conversavam
Nada
Um copo de conhaque
Um teatro
Um precipício
Talvez o precipicio queira dizer nada
Uma carteirinha de travel's check
Uma partida for two nada
Trouxeram-me camélias brancas e vermelhas
Uma linda criança sorriume quando eu a abraçava
Um cão rosnava na minha estrada
Um papagaio falava coisas tão engraçadas
Pastorinhas entraram em meu caminho
Num samba morenamente cadenciado
Abri o meu abraço aos amigos de sempre
Poetas compareceram
Alguns escritores
Gente de teatro
Birutas no aeroporto
E nada.

Nothing

Nada nada nada
Nothing but nothing
Because you want scarcely nothing to exist
Since only nothing exists
A shattered windscreen a broken leg
A nothing
Cruel disfigurement
Friends' arms in slings
Doors battered open
Opening onto nothing
An infant's sobbing
A streetwalker's tear
Signifying nothing
A half-darkened room
A lamp with broken shade
Girls who danced
who chatted
Nothing
A glass of cognac
A theater
A precipice
Possibly the precipice means nothing
A little folder of traveller's checks
A game for two—nothing
They have brought me camelias white and red
A pretty baby smiled at me when I hugged her
A dog snarled on the road
A parrot spoke such witty lines
Girls in shepherd's guise joined the parade
In a darkly cadenced samba
I offered my embrace to my most constant friends
Poets showed up
Some writers
Theater people
Loonies at the airport
And nothing

JOSÉ EMILIO PACHECO

ARBOL ENTRE DOS MUROS
TREE BETWEEN TWO WALLS

Sitiado entre dos noches
(entre dos multitudes cuyo pacto
un mismo sonido deshilvana y recubre;
entre dos pozos, dos cuencas arrasadas
de sorda agua que espera;
entre dos cielos que corren a su alcance;
dos cantiles roídos que suelen despeñarse en sus hoscas mitades;
dos cadenas de espejos, navegables murallas;
dos bestias aladas que se muerden la cola),
el día esplende, gira sobre su aire y su memoria,
deja caer sus fechas, sus ciudades, sus rostros.
Alza—caballero impaciente, ángel desmoronado—
su enorme espada de claridad;
su espada como un mar de luz que se levanta afilándose,
como un vaso sin labios que contuviera el espesor del mundo,
como un tallo que embiste contra el marfil de esta pregunta
    inerme
—ojo devorador, fiesta carnívora en la espesura del reloj al
    minuto.

Atrás, combate el tiempo contra el cielo,
como algo que no acaba al apagarse,
un arpa sin sonido en la que el aire tañe su desgaste;
la señal devorada por el musgo y el agua al pie de la llanura;
el gran árbol que fluye
sobre la veta móvil de su gran río de savia,
el muro de tinieblas
donde abandona el mundo nuestro nombre enlazado;
el final de la hoguera
—largo fuego de bruces comiendo sus destellos—
pero es invulnerable—saqueo, amplia derrota—
porque todo termina encima de la noche . . .

Trapped between two nights
(between two armies who unthread and rewind
the unending sound of their reciprocal guarantee;
between two pits, two waiting basins
tense with water dull to the edge;
between two skies rushing together;
two eroded cliffs that throw themselves by habit down into
    crabbed stark halves;
two chains of mirrors, grand navigable walls;
two winged beasts each biting the other's tail),
the day shines,
turns on its air and its memory;
lets fall its dates, its cities, its faces.
The day—prompt horseman, flaking angel—
raises its great sword of clarity;
its sword a sea of light which rises keenly,
like a cup lips never touch and in it the concentration of the world,
or the flower stem which rams the marble of this defenceless question
—devouring eye, carnivorous fiesta in the thickness of the clock
    upon the minute.

Behind us, time fights against the sky
like a snuffed thing that flickers beyond its ending,
a harp without sound on which the wind plays the tune of its own
    wear;
the blaze darkened by the moss and water at the foot of the
    plateau;
the great tree flowing
on the moving lode of its fluency of sap,
the wall of darkness
where the world abandons our entwined name;
the end of the burning
—this long slow fire ingesting its own brilliancies face
    downward—
but it is invulnerable
                        —despoilation, sweeping defeat—
because everything ends above the night ...

Porque todo se extingue sobre ti, bahía insólita,
riente arboleda donde sepulta el trueno su rezongo.
Como incendiada hiedra sobre ti misma creces,
como el cristal te miras en tu yerta blancura.

Entonces, cuando el día impenetrable y hueco
comienza a levantarse y repta y ríe
dejo caer tu nombre:
haz de letras impávidas que suenan a río huraño.
Y de tu nombre surgen la luna y su claro linaje;
pero tu nombre llega lacio y gastado como una promisión que no
    se cumple,
como espejismo que ha zarpado de los ojos en ruinas,
como una isla vencida que brilla y se consume:
parda moneda que escondí en el aire.

Pero ese rostro, torre que atalayaba el agua del estío, era tu rostro,
tumba de huecos vivos en la que el mundo excava un testimonio
mientras ronda una noche abandonada, en cada valle,
en cada almena del espacio
que surca un mismo viento.

Todo es claro, amor mío;
todo es el huracán y el viento que huye:
todo nos interroga y recrimina.
Pero nada responde,
nada persiste y se alza contra el viaje del día,
el sol se desvincula y ya no late y es un clamor desértico;
cada resurrección es una afrenta
y despertar es corromper un sueño.

Mientras avanza, el día se devora
y sus ruinas se esparcen sobre un reino asolado.

Because everything is extinguished upon you, strange shore,
smiling plantation, where the thunder buries its sounding.
Like burning ivy you scale yourself,
reflect, like crystal, your inflexible whiteness.

Then, when the impenetrable and hollow day
begins to rise and snakes and laughs,
then I let fall your name:
a sheaf of roman letters which like a wild river sound.
And from your name the moon and its splendid lineage rise;
but your name reaches me lank and used, an unkept promise,
a delusion which has sailed out from eyes in ruins,
a conquered island which flares and is consumed:
a dull coin I hid in the air.

But that face, a tower which watched over the water of summer
      was your face,
a tomb of hollow quicknesses in which the world
      excavates a testament
while an abandoned night pays court, in each valley,
in each crenelation of the space
that unchanging wind ploughs.

Everything is clear my love;
everything is the hurricane and the fleeing wind;
everything interrogates and accuses us.
But nothing answers,
nothing persists, nothing rises against the journey of the day,
the sun is unwound and no longer pulses and is a cry in the desert;
each resurrection is an insult
and to awake is to corrupt a dream.

The day is consumed in its progression
and its ruins are spread over a scorched demesne.

Mas tú, señora, creces sobre ese largo acatamiento,
sobre el filo desnudo de ese acontecer que nos llega de lejos,
de algún cielo agrietado en el que el orden
comienza a pisotear las desangradas piedras.

El día pasa por mi frente como el oleaje encorva el pensamiento;
cuando camina se envejece, y yo miro su espalda,
sus pies hendidos de romero y galeote, su huella encadenada
hasta tocar los soles que vencen al abismo.

Y mientras viaja el día hasta las rojas puertas
—límites del castigo, fronteras donde acaba toda permanencia—
muestra la noche su luz, su don, su cabellera en llamas,
su lengua que todo mancha de tiniebla,
su rostro que ya no mira nadie;
brusco río que toma alas
y asciende a derribar los ojos de sus reinos hipnóticos.
Combate y sueña en su fluvial dominio
—manantial que se absorbe en la hora que rema
hasta hundirse en un párpado.

But you, Señora, thrive on this long obeisance,
on the bare edge of this occurrence which reaches us from the
    distance,
from some riddled sky in which order
is beginning to crush the bloodless stones.

The day passes over my forehead just as the sea warps thought;
walking, the day grows old and I look at its back,
its broken palmer's feet, galleyslave's feet, its footstep chained
until it touches the suns who conquer the abyss.

And while the day journeys to the red gateways
—the extremes of punishment, frontiers where all permanency
    ends—
the night displays its light, its gift, its hair ablaze,
its tongue which stains all things with darkness,
its face no one any longer looks upon;
a river-spate it is which takes wings
and rises to tear down eyes from their hypnotic demesnes.
Night wars and dreams in its fluvial territory
—a wellspring absorbed into the hour which oars on
until it is sunk in an eyelid.

Endnotes to *Modern Chronicles*

César Vallejo

From *César Vallejo: Selected Poems* (Penguin: Harmondsworth, 1976), which drew on *Los heraldos negros* (1919), *Trilce* (1922), *Poemas humanos* (1923–38, published posthumously) and *España, aparta de mi este cáliz* (1938). "Telúrica y magnética" was translated especially for this volume.

137. Drawing of César Vallejo by Pablo Picasso.

140. Manuel González Prada: renowned Peruvian socialist and atheist (1848–1918).

153. "otiline veins" (Trilce VI): from the proper name Otilia; Vallejo parted from a woman of this name in 1919.

163. "cell" (Trilce XVIII): this is one of the Trilce poems which refers to Vallejo's three and a half months in prison in Trujillo on a charge of arson that was never proved.

163. "four corners tear/out daily rusted limbs" (Trilce XVIII): this recalls the fate of Tupac Amaru II, deeply implanted in Quechua and Andean memory. A descendant of the last Inca Tupac Amaru I, this hero threw the Spaniards out of the highlands in 1780—only to be captured, and quartered in Cuzco by horses tugging his limbs in four directions.

165. "M. Jean Jacques" (Trilce XXII): the 18th-century French philosopher Jean-Jacques Rousseau, attacked by his contemporaries for being solitary and sentimental.

219. "Calderón ... Cervantes ... Quevedo ... Santa Teresa": all figures from the literature of Spain's "Golden Age," the high point of that country's imperial power. As a citizen of Peru, an ex-colony, Vallejo discovers subversion in these writers, one which is taken up subsequently by Coll, Goya, Cajal, and the celebrated revolutionary of the Spanish Civil War, Lina Odena.

Patricia Galvão

From *Album de Pagú* (1929) with later poems originally published in *A Tribuna*, the Santos newspaper (1960–2); included in Augusto de Campos, *Pagu: Vida-Obra* (Brasiliense: São Paulo, 1982). These translations were done in collaboration with Lúcia Sá, especially for this volume.

237. Album: the original has 28 framed and numbered entries, most of which are illustrated. Twelve of them are selected here.

249. "Go see if I'm around the corner" means "piss off." Being "on the corner" means soliciting.

José Emilio Pacheco
From *Tree between Two Walls* (Black Sparrow Press: Los Angeles, 1968). The original poem, "Arbol entre dos muros" was first published in *Los elementos de la noche* (UNAM: Mexico, 1963).

A professor in the Creative Writing/English department at the University of Colorado, Boulder, Edward Dorn is the author of a socio-anthropological study, *The Shoshoneans: The People of the Basin Plateau* (William Morrow & Co., 1966), a novel, *By the Sound* (Frontier Press, 1968), *Gunslinger* (1967–74), *Recollections of Gran Apachería* (1974), *Collected Poems* (1956–75), *Abhorrences* (1990) and *Way West: Stories, Essays and Verse Accounts* (1963–1993). He has been the recipient of a Fulbright Lectureship, University of Essex (1965–67); a D. H. Lawrence Fellowship; an American Book Award, 1980, and an American Book Award for Life Time Achievement (1989).

Gordon Brotherston is currently research professor at the University of Essex and Professor at Indiana University, Bloomington. He helped to set up the Latin American program at the newly-opened University of Essex in 1965, and has devoted his interest to the indigenous cultures which flourished for thousands of years before Columbus. He is the author of *Latin American Poetry: Origins and Presence* (Cambridge University Press, 1975) and *The Emergence of the Latin American Novel* (Cambridge University Press, 1977), and numerous publications on the native texts of Mesoamerica, including *Image of the New World* (Thames & Hudson, London, 1979), *Book of the Fourth World* (Cambridge University Press, 1992), and *Painted Books from Mexico* (British Museum Press, 1995). For his work he has been awarded fellowships from the Alexander von Humboldt Stiftung, the British Academy, and the Guggenheim Foundation.